Stepping Out

A GUIDE TO SHORT TERM MISSIONS

Originally Edited and Compiled
by Tim Gibson
Steve Hawthorne
Richard Krekel
Kn Moy

YWAM PUBLISHING
A Ministry Of Youth With A Mission
P.O. Box 55787, Seattle, WA 98155

Stepping Out

Published by
YWAM Publishing
P. O. Box 55787
Seattle, WA 98155

(A Division of Youth With A Mission)

ISBN 0-92754-529-2

Printed in the United States of America

Why *Stepping Out?*

In 1986, approximately 60,000 North Americans served the Lord all over the world on short-term missions. That's ten times the number that went out ten years before. God is developing a short-term mission movement that can encourage, enable, and assist the Church in its growth worldwide.

You might be saying, "I want to be involved!" But you may also be asking, "What can I do that will be significant? Who would I talk to? What kind of mission organization can I trust? Who works in China? Who does something in Africa? Are they financially sound? Are they biblical?"

That's why we created *Stepping Out: A Guide to Short-Term Missions.*

Stepping Out will help you to:

- *examine* what God is saying to you about how He wants to use you;
- *search* for a mission organization that can help involve you in a short-term mission experience;
- *think* about preparation and training;
- *care* for yourself on the field; and
- *integrate* this whole process into your life.

Stepping Out originated as a research project at World Vision, and then took shape through the efforts of The Fellowship of Short-Term Mission Leaders, which meets annually in Colorado Springs, Colorado.

We owe a debt of gratitude to World Vision for backing this publication. We especially thank Dr. Ted Engstrom for his encouragement and support and Tim Gibson, the chairman of the original *Stepping Out* Development Committee, as well as the original editorial and production team of Steve Hawthorne, Kn Moy, and Rick Krekel for their hard work. Finally, special thanks goes to the Fellowship of Short-Term Missions Leaders and the board of its auxiliary, Short-Term Missions Advocates.

Jim Rogers
YWAM Publishing
Lindale, Texas

A Long-term Leader
Looks at Short-term Missions

By John Kyle

John Kyle, former director of the Urbana conventions in the 1980s, is presently serving as the executive director of Mission to the World, the overseas sending agency of the Presbyterian Church in America.

You march to a different drumbeat. You've heard Jesus Christ's command to move in new directions. As an echo of that command, the very title *Stepping Out* is a call to action.

This is a significant publication, aimed directly at those Christians who think they might go on a short-term missionary journey, and to the individuals in local churches across North America who will stand behind them.

The ministry short-term missionaries have accomplished and will accomplish is tremendous. Thousands of lost people have been led to Christ, career missionaries have been encouraged by having others at their side, spiritual battles have been fought, buildings have been built, and airstrips have been constructed.

This is a modern-day phenomenon—or, if you please, a modern-day miracle—never before seen in history. Think of God's multiplication of laborers from the original Twelve He sent out for *their* first short-term mission. Now they're joined by thousands of others from around the world.

My generation of Americans had its short-term experience during World War II. We saw the world beyond North America and the tragic needs of people everywhere. Later, many thousands went out as career missionaries.

Christians need to see that a giant for the cause of Christ is striding among us. It's called the short-term missionary movement. As you read the articles in this publication, you might sense a desire to become involved yourself. You may say, "I could be a short-term missionary. Why not step out?"

I've been privileged to be close to the genesis of *Stepping Out*. Ten years ago, two young men who are close to me got deeply involved in short-term missions. I urged them to gather an ad hoc meeting for young people involved in sending out short-term missionaries. A new generation of young people involved in missions now meets each year to further the cause of the short term.

One of these two men has begun an organization to help self-supporting missionaries get into so-called closed countries. The other now leads a church-planting team as a career missionary. He is my son, and was a short-term missionary years ago. He's one example of the effect that a short-term mission can have.

Today, thousands of people go out to serve Christ for a couple of weeks or a couple of years. Short-term missions are the *gateway* to career missionary service. With modern means of travel and a Christian community in many nations that has been greatly blessed with strong churches, we can see a new wave of career missionaries developing through their short-term experience.

Short terms are a way for you to "test the waters." They also give the local church and sending agencies a way to gauge if a person is truly fitted for long-term overseas service. Short terms are happening in the face of the fact that there are now over five billion people in the world, half of whom have never heard the Gospel in an understandable manner. The grim reality is that many of those who went overseas as career missionaries in that great wave of missionaries after World War II will soon be retiring.

As you read the articles in this handbook, please prayerfully consider not only how God might want you to serve Him on a short-term mission, but also how a short term might become the gateway to a career of missionary work. Lay some plans and begin some new habits with the long view in mind. Consider how you can help others begin missionary work as a result of your short-term involvement. Build relationships now with people who can counsel you later. Get to know some missionaries. Pray for the world. Start a journal. Investigate opportunities for service that you can come back to for a career.

The key, once you step out, is to keep moving. *Stepping Out* will not only help you on your short-term adventure, but will also help you to keep thinking and acting in world missions. This will keep missions burning in your heart.

Jesus Christ has set no limitations as to how His Gospel will get out around the world or who will go with it. He only says to Christians, "You will be my witnesses in Jerusalem, and in all Judea and Samaria, and to the ends of the earth" (Acts 1:8). He tells us clearly that "this gospel of the kingdom will be preached in the whole world as a testimony to all nations, and then the end will come" (Matt. 24:14). I invite you to step out toward the ends of the earth as He brings us to the end of the age.

Table of Contents

Go!

Making the most of a short term. Gearing your expectations for reality.

Going On....

User's Guide—Use *Stepping Out* as a...

Guide

The decisions you face are probably complex. Don't look for easy answers. *Stepping Out* avoids a wooden list of steps or programmed flow charts. Most articles can help you to think through some fresh options or look at things a bit differently. Every article tries to boil down years of experience into a few wise words.

You'll find items called "Checkpoints," designed to help you work through issues and decisions about your short term. These appear as tests or quizzes, but there are no right or wrong answers. They're merely inventories and self-examinations which can help you understand where you stand on certain issues or decisions.

If you are just opening up the missions issue in your life and aren't sure what you think or feel, start with the first article and continue on by browsing through the book.

If you have been involved for some time in missions work, or if you have the help of someone who has, dip in the book anywhere and keep ransacking the articles for the help you need.

Resource

No matter how experienced or inexperienced you might be in missions work, *Stepping Out* can offer you some fresh ideas and easy-to-use information.

This book isn't organized in dictionary style. Any particular issue may appear in several places. Start with the Table of Contents on page 7. Be sure to use the Index on page 215 to find references on a certain topic. To wring out every idea in *Stepping Out*, you're going to have to keep rummaging through every article.

Discussion starter

Whether you're part of a church, school, or mission group, select and discuss articles together and use the checkpoints to prompt conversation and help you work through issues you are facing together. The following plan of study will help a group or team prepare together for a short-term mission.

Read "Maximum Short-term Mission" on page 83 and use these five points as themes for five sessions.

Session One: Extend. "Why are we going on a short term?"

Before the group session, read "A Call for Ordinary People" on page 17, the article by John Kyle on page 5, and "Not Thirsty, Still Hungry" on page 27.

Discuss what you discovered from John four about why anyone should go on a short term. Discuss the balance of personal growth for yourself and the advance of God's kingdom which may result from your expedition. Read "Motive Mix" on page 31.

Session Two: Expose. "How can we involve our church or fellowship in our short-term mission?"

Before coming to the session, read: "Make the Right Connections" on page 47 and one of the three articles beginning on page 59 ("Bridge Building," "Get Blessed," and "Honoring Parents"). Decide on specific ways to get others involved early in the process. Read the articles about support raising on pages 71 to 79 before getting together. Consider the passages Roger Randall suggests for further study. Discuss how the principles he mentions affect your own feelings about support raising. Review Chris Stanton's suggestions. Plan together how to develop your individual strategies. Think of ways to help each other.

Session Three: Experience. "How can we prepare for the cultural differences we'll encounter?"

Read "Great Expectations" on page 143 and other articles of interest from the *Go!* section before meeting. Consider the guidelines mentioned in "Culture Clash" on page 145. Take turns describing what you imagine your short term will be like. Use the checkpoint on page 166 to make a list of anticipations. How can you be realistic and yet expect great things from God?

Session Four: Exchange. "How can we build good relationships with nationals and other team members while overseas?"

Before meeting, select three articles to pre-read from the series on relationships which starts on page 89 and continues to page 132. Discuss how the principles described in the articles may help you grow as you relate to team members. Anticipate the partnerships you can enjoy with nationals. What difficulties can you expect? What heart attitudes should you have in order to serve well?

Session Five: Explore. "What vision might God give us to use our lives for His glory overseas or at home?"

Before meeting, read "Growing as World Christians" on page 191, "The Homecoming" on page 175, and "Looking Ahead" on page 195. Identify ways you can prepare for your return before you leave. Talk about your feelings regarding your future. How would you know God wanted you to work in missions longer term? Read and discuss "Writers Keepers" on page 137 and encourage each other to keep journals during your experience.

Where are You in *Stepping Out?*

Ready?

"I'm exploring if a short-term mission experience is for me."

- Start with the three articles in the *Ready?* section, beginning on page 15.

- Be sure to use the worksheet called "Motive Mix" on page 31.

- Sample the articles which tell more of what you can expect on a short-term: "Opening the World" on page 35, "Maximum Short-Term Mission" on page 83, or "Great Expectations" on page 143. Have fun with "Expectation Check" on page 166.

- Think through the heart issues driving you or holding you back: "Winning by Losing" on page 93, "Looking Ahead" on page 195, or "God's Pattern of Provision" on page 71.

Get Set.

"I'm definitely going on a short term. Now I'm deciding where and when I should go."

- Begin with articles starting on page 33.

- If you're having a hard time knowing what you want in a short term, note "Discovering the Best Short-Term Mission" on page 41 and the worksheet called "Decision Points" on page 46.

- Bring key people and your church into your decision making. Find out how to do this in the articles on pages 47 to 77.

"I've decided on my mission opportunity. Right now I'm preparing for the experience."

- You may want to start with a general article like "Preparation" on page 153 or "Maximum Short-Term Mission" on page 83.

- The entire *Go!* section is designed to help you to prepare in some important ways. Try reading straight through pages 81 to 171. Or pick through this section, focusing on your greatest needs.

Go!

"I'm in the field on a short-term mission. I need ideas about how to handle some specific problems."

- Much of the *Go!* section will make the most sense to someone on the field. Think carefully through each article on pages 81 to 171 early in your short term.

- Don't wait until you have problems with relationships to apply some of the ideas in the articles on pages 89 to 132.

- It's not too soon to begin thinking about what will happen when you return home. Consider some of the issues mentioned on pages 175 to 214.

- Disappointment may be hitting you hard. Review your expectations. Reconsider some of the thoughts in "Culture Clash" on page 145 and "Great Expectations" on page 143.

Going On....

"I've returned home from my short-term experience. Everything seems so different. What do I do now? How can I serve further?"

- Prepare to come home even before you leave. Scan the entire section called *Going On....* Pick out certain ideas to implement before taking off.

- Think through your future. Scrutinize your life plans and ambitions using the articles, "Looking Ahead" on page 195 and "Not Thirsty, Still Hungry" on page 27.

- Consider seriously making missions work a career. Try the worksheet on page 213. Implement some of the ideas in "Linking Up for Life" on page 207.

- Don't let the experience get stale. Work hard at integrating your short-term effort into the flow of your daily life. Start with "Growing as World Christians" on page 191 for some ideas.

Ready?

Are you ready for a short-term experience? You may not see yourself as a "missionary," but there may be ways you never imagined to serve God in a different culture.

1

A Call for Ordinary People

The incredible possibilities of short-term service

by Douglas Millham

Douglas Millham seeks to build bridges of understanding between churches in the U.S. and developing countries as director and co-founder of Discover the World, Inc.

I see signs that God is raising an army of ordinary people of every age and background. They are willing to follow Him across cultural boundaries and international borders to spread His love. Never in history have there been so many creative, exciting opportunities to serve the Lord. Never has it been so easy to discover what God is doing and become a part of it.

If Not Now, When?

We may be breaking into a new era in mission history in which short-term ministries will flood the nations. According to some estimates, the number of short-termers from the U.S.A. grew tenfold from about 6,000 in 1975 to over 60,000 in 1987.

You only have to look at groups like Youth With A Mission (YWAM) to see the explosion. Started in 1960 as an evangelistic outreach program for younger people, YWAM now fields more than 20,000 short-term volunteers of every age and background each year. They are engaged in the most creative and diversified ministries you can imagine. In 1991 they completed their goal of sending ministry to every nation on earth with an indigenous population as a team traveled to Pitcairn Island.

More than 350 mission agencies send short-termers. Hundreds of churches or whole denominations in North America offer opportunities in short-term missions. For a follower of Christ today, the possibilities for short-term ministry are quite astounding.

What is a Short-Term Mission?

Some define short-term missions as any service overseas or cross-culturally from two weeks to two years or more. What is a short-termer? A willing servant. A committed Christian of any age.

He or she is usually not making a career decision, but stepping out of a career path to serve God's global cause.

The locations and types of short-term ministry are as varied as the people who go out on them. Many augment the efforts of career missionaries by serving alongside them. Others go out in specialized teams for select projects. Others find ways to use their careers, student years, or military service in other cultures as opportunities for Christian witness. Even three-week vacations are being used for the Gospel. There are few countries where short-term efforts haven't been made. In fact, in many countries, a short stay is all that governments will allow.

Of course, the mission task is complex. The evangelization of the unreached will need more and more people called and committed to entire lifetimes of mission service. Career translators, church planters, evangelists, teachers, and trainers are all desperately needed throughout the world. But at the same time, the short-term movement of our day just could be God's chosen means for this complex mission of the Church to expand in ways that traditional missions never imagined.

It's a Changing Ministry

Creative and different ministries are capturing people for the cause that probably would not have been involved otherwise. And these people tend to find new angles to serve. Tony Campolo challenged a recent group of Harvard M.B.A.'s: "Anybody can get a great job at IBM and be a success. How many of you can go to Haiti and start a cooperative bakery among the poor?" Six went, and their summer will change the lives of hundreds.

There are even opportunities to work among the nearly 85 percent of all non-Christians in the world who live in countries which cannot be entered by people with "missionary" stamped in their passport. One leader with Campus Crusade for Christ said, "In countries that limit missionary visas, we can send in students as tourists. Sure, they won't speak the language, but they can help show a film on the life of Jesus that's dubbed with the local language." There, in partnership with national Christian leaders, the short-term person gives much needed support and receives invaluable exposure to a world of mission.

It's a Changing Church

In many countries, the national Church leadership is emerging to a point of independence and strength which is greater than ever. In Korea, Kenya, India, Japan, and dozens of other places around the world, there is an explosion of cross-cultural missions by these relatively young Christian churches. In many cases these expanding churches work closely with some of the hundreds of short-term mission agencies. They rely upon them to provide willing servants who will come and help with some type of technical, pastoral, or professional skill.

But It's the Same Need

Last I heard, God hadn't recalled the Great Commission. Two-thirds of the world still is waiting to hear the Gospel, and most of them don't yet have any way out of the frightful darkness of poverty and injustice that refuses to go away. And Jesus promised to send help to them, *through His followers*. That's you and that's me, friends. What a privilege. What an opportunity.

If Not Me, Who?

You'll find plenty of short-term opportunities available. Some short-term programs are extremely well planned, the training and preparation are excellent, and the field experience is meaningful for both the host and the participants. Standards of excellence vary, so choose carefully.

But the place to start is not the menu of programs. Rather, take a good look at yourself. The list isn't going anywhere, and neither should you until you have taken inventory of your motives and your heart. Look closely at your skills, interests, abilities, and feelings. This will help you sort out your thoughts and help others to offer guidance.

But also look beyond yourself. Always keep the big picture in view: God is doing something phenomenal in His world today, and you just may want to be a part of it.

Wanted: Garden-Variety Christians

My own decision to try a short-term experience didn't come to me as any great revelation, no booming voice. It was just a moment in my life when I thought about one simple thing: if Christ gave His life for an ordinary person like me, then maybe if I give it back, He can do something extraordinary with it.

I did have one major hang-up, however. I'd also been aiming my life to be one filled with excitement, adventure, and travel. I wanted a chance to meet lots of people and contribute something meaningful to the world. Little did I realize at the time that those very goals would be expanded and fulfilled beyond my wildest dreams through a short-term mission experience.

One day a few years ago, I turned on my TV and was stunned, yet strangely fascinated, by what I saw. A news report out of East Africa showed scenes of human suffering that melted my heart. I picked up the phone, and six months later I found myself living in a tent in a refugee camp in Somalia, trying to do anything I could to help bring a little joy to a frightful situation. I returned home a year later as a person completely transformed, totally committed to a life of service to others.

I wasn't the most likely candidate for a short term, but between 1981 and 1985, my wife Jackie and I lived overseas, first in Somalia and then in Thailand. We worked for a Christian organization, taught the Bible, and communicated the Gospel as best we could. We had the privilege to introduce Muslims, Buddhists, and all kinds of people to the love of Jesus Christ.

We hadn't thought of ourselves as missionary types. But we were actively seeking God's guidance for a challenge and a future, for a choice of direction we could take which would make a difference in this world. He gave us a choice, and we took it. It's as simple as that. We're not heroic people. We see ourselves as garden-variety Christians who had such a tremendous experience during a one-year short term that we stayed on for more.

Perhaps you feel heroic. *Seeds* magazine (Oct.'85) said it best: "It's okay to be idealistic; that's probably why you're thinking about volunteering in the first place. But if you plan on saving the world, or even one village or neighborhood, watch out. At best, you can be a part of the solution, an agent of change. But you can hardly expect as a short- or even long-term volunteer to reverse decades of poverty, inequality, racism, or pain." So let's be realistic. In a sense, we go to test ourselves, to see what we are made of and what we can do in this world. Honest, realistic motives like these can be used by God if given totally into His hands.

Do You Have What it Takes?

You might be surprised to find out how ready you are. In reviewing candidates for our short-term programs, we look for four basic things. Examine yourself in light of the following characteristics. Are you reaching for them, even though you may not be where you would like to be? If so, you may be a good candidate for a short-term experience.

1. Mature in personal faith. There are a lot of different levels and styles of spiritual maturity. None of us is quite the same as any other. In the end, you alone can judge your own maturity in Christ.

When you look at yourself for possible short-term ministry, begin by taking a very basic self-examination. Ask yourself, "Am I confident of my salvation through a personal faith in Jesus Christ as my Lord and Savior?" Your walk with Him must be strong and growing. Daily devotions, quiet times, a personal prayer life, and Christian fellowship can be external indicators of a mature life in Christ.

2. Motivated to serve and learn. There's only room for one Savior on this earth. And neither you nor I are that one. We must not go into the world believing we can save it. Only Christ can do that. But we can spread His healing love as men and women who go into other cultures and nations willing to learn from others, to serve beside them in whatever way the Holy Spirit of God guides.

3. Committed to work in Christian community. Jesus had a reason for sending His disciples out two by two. Men and women in ministry need the accountability, strength, and fellowship of others. There is no room for the Lone Ranger type individual in the short-term environment. Only team players need apply. The excitement, the stresses and strains, and the blessings and joys all require the strength and unity of the Body of Christ. The key here is to be sure that you are vitally linked with other Christians now.

4. Skilled socially or professionally. A great deal of the ministry of the Church around the world is lived out in acts of love and care for those in need. Many children's homes, orphanages, schools, and communities cry out for people who will simply come and spend time with them, hugging babies, weeping with those who weep, celebrating life with those who seem to have little to celebrate, bringing that cold cup of water in new and creative ways.

Can you communicate lovingly? You may not learn another language fluently during a short term, but are you ready to reach out to people you haven't met before to offer whatever words you can? You may not be called on to preach sermons, but are you ready for the hard work of communicating with people different from you? The greatest compliment which could be given to you overseas might be that you are a "people" person, eager to meet the challenge of new and interesting social situations every day.

There is no question, however, that persons skilled in technical specialties are in high demand all around the world. And those who go with a servant heart seem to be welcomed back a second time. You will find that many agencies seeking short-term volunteers will list skill requirements for specialists in health, agriculture, medicine, carpentry, water, community development, evangelism, and many other areas. If you lack such skills, but possess all the other attributes and attitudes, don't let this stop you. Most short-termers are amazed at the skills they develop while overseas.

Step Out

Give yourself the opportunity of a lifetime, and don't let old impressions hold you back. Many of us have seen missionaries at our churches and have said, "That will never be me." Why? Because we have outdated images of the types of people who are involved in missions. After all, it's common to think that missionaries are either super-spiritual oddities or losers in the real world who turned to Christian service after failing.

Set aside your old images. Forget your childhood stereotypes of missionaries. Instead, look into the eyes of Jesus and ask Him if He wants you to join Him in doing a new thing in the world.

Unlike the Marines, who are "looking for a few good men," our Lord is actively recruiting, right now, tens of thousands of *ordinary* men and women, just like you and me. God is looking into the hearts of His followers and seeking those with passion for making Christ known. He is calling them to walk with Him into the world. He is looking for ordinary people, but people with a vision for what God can do if we believe Him. He is looking for people with a willingness to carry the claims of Christ "to the ends of the earth" (Acts 1:8).

Don't walk around in circles looking for small successes. Instead, take a single, simple, short step in the right direction. Step out. Step out into the incredible possibilities that await you in short-term ministry.

2

Does it Work?

Why short terms cause more good than harm

by Greg Livingstone

Greg Livingstone helped launch the short-term movement with Operation Mobilisation. He now leads Frontiers, a movement of career church-planting teams among Muslim peoples.

We called it "Operation Mobilisation," rallying 2,000 young people from 20 countries to visit every village in Austria, Belgium, France, Italy, and Spain. It sounded exciting to many students in the early '60s, but it sounded like bunk to many others. As fast as I could get out the challenge to minister for a summer in Europe, the criticisms came pouring in.

"How can you waste money which was sacrificed for missions on a summer campaign? That money could go to real career missionaries," chided our accusers. This reproof sent me, the 22-year-old U.S. coordinator for O.M., off to see Dr. Don Hillis, then the general director of TEAM in Wheaton, Illinois. Hillis understood something: God is behind a lot of efforts that, though they initially may not look all that strategic, are somehow part of God's process.

Actually, short terms are a lot more strategic than they first seem. People say that they're waste of money, that they promote a lack of commitment, that they don't help the cause of world evangelization, and that they just plain cause more harm than good. But take a closer look.

Are They a Waste?

First, look at the *money* argument. Today we live life in the "fast lane" in our global village. Casablanca is only six hours from New York. Travel has never been cheaper. William Carey, an influential missionary in the 1700s, spent the equivalent of today's $400,000 to get passage for his family *one way* to India. That's 20 times the average Christian's annual salary today.

Besides the fact that short terms are relatively inexpensive, to worry about short-termers using money that would otherwise go to career missionaries is to think in terms of the limited-pie theory. This reasoning says that there's only so much mission money around, so it isn't fair or wise to take it from career missionaries. I think studies would show that short-termers often earn a large portion of their funds before going, or receive money that wouldn't normally be designated to other missionaries.

Short terms often boost the vision of the local church. It's one thing to hear about missionaries; it's another thing to have your own Suzie going to Kuala Lumpur. Churches end up giving more to missions in the long run.

What Can They Do?

Short terms expose people to the needs of the world—effectively. Operation Mobilisation has seen more than 30,000 young people go on short-term teams from a month to two years in Mexico, Italy, Belgium, France, Israel, the Arab world, India, Pakistan, Bangladesh, and Indonesia. Some estimate that 50 percent of the career missionaries in Italy today first came there as summer workers with O.M.

But are all these short-termers of any use while they're getting their first taste of ministry overseas? Summer teams in Spain in 1963 convinced the government of Madrid to give the Protestants a freedom they'd wanted for decades. When Spanish believers saw Americans and northern Europeans willing to go to jail for distributing Bibles across the cities of Spain, many took on a new courage to stand for Christ.

Some ministries will always require people committed for life. But short-termers have proven helpful. In most situations, short-termers can't effectively plant churches by themselves. But they can help. During my years with Operation Mobilisation, it was common for a team of 20 young people to spend a summer with a church-planting missionary. They were usually able to find more interested people in one month than the missionary could ferret out in five years. Then the missionary could give all his time to following up on those interested in the Gospel. Short-termers, then, can accelerate the ministries of the career missionaries.

Dedication Deadlock

Some wonder if short-termers are merely salving their evangelical conscience or appeasing their denomination. They wonder if short-termers go with no intention to stay, but go merely to grit their teeth and get their two years of missionary work out of the way so that they can do what they want to do afterward.

That's not been true in my experience of recruiting for missions for more than 25 years. I've met very few short-termers who, like young Mormons, are going out because of a guilt complex or family pressure. Most aren't trying to arrange a deferment to avoid God's draft for lifetime commitment. Instead, they're usually seeking the Lord's face for a longer assignment. Many conclude correctly that they may not be appropriately gifted to be a cross-cultural disciple-maker or that they're really not ready to cope with living in another culture unmarried. That's an important discovery to make.

I often overhear old-timers regret out loud that young people today simply aren't dedicated. "They aren't ready to commit themselves to the mission field until age 65," they say. They remember the days when missionaries would go for life and never come back.

Actually, this generation may be more in touch with its feelings than generations gone by and can more easily say, "I don't know." People today simply don't hear God saying, "Give your life to Africa." They struggle to understand how they can best invest the next few years to accomplish God's purposes. They figure God will show them later what is His later agenda. "How do you know if you're supposed to serve in Pakistan if you've never been there?" Good question, I think.

How do people really know if they'll have the grace to cope in the country of Mali where it can hit 130 degrees? Or if they can minister with joy as a single person among Albanian Muslims in Yugoslavia? Who knows for sure? "Go give it a shot, and if the Lord wants you to keep going, I'm confident you'll obey Him," I advise today's candidates.

A short term can help anyone test his or her strengths in the rigors and cost of mission work. One of the dangers of the new generation, which lets it "all hang out," is that people can too quickly limit themselves to their weaknesses and figure that they don't have what it takes, when perhaps they really do—by God's grace. If you're going to be honest about your weaknesses, be sure to be just as honest about God's strength. God's strength is made perfect in weakness.

Once, missions was an all-or-nothing question. Now people who couldn't—or wouldn't—consider a lifetime overseas take short stints abroad. That's great, because we tend to get a burden for people we've walked among, or touched, or laughed with. Perhaps missions is still all or nothing. It's hard to catch God's heart for all the world if you've known nothing but your own hometown.

I wish every American Christian could see, smell, feel, and walk in the streets of Bombay or Cairo or Jakarta. No churches on every corner there. No evidence of witnessing Christians. Statistics don't do it, but looking into the faces of multitudes of Hindus and Muslims, so thick on Bombay's sidewalks you can hardly move, does. Nothing is so effective in molding a career world Christian.

My own son, David, was shoving his way through the crowded market of Fez, Morocco, a few years ago when he began to mumble, "It isn't fair."

"What?" I asked.

"It isn't fair—these people have no way to hear about Jesus."

"That's why I'm in the missions business, son." I looked up at God and smiled as I saw the light go on and compassion fill my son's eyes.

Take a Risk

That's my plea in a sentence. Be like the adventurous servant in the parable of the talents (Matt. 25:14-30). How will you face God at the end of August, or a year from now? Will you reluctantly unscrew your fist and show him the single talent, earthy from having been buried, creased from having been clenched secretly and tightly in your hand? Or will you bring handfuls of talents, risked, speculated, yet doubled and tripled through a summer or a year of adventurous faith?

Gambling your life in Christ's service is not so reckless as it seems. It would be if God were incompetent or foolish or simply not quite able to cope with things anymore. But in recklessly throwing yourself into His hands, you are putting yourself in the charge of the sovereign Lord of the universe, the One who speaks and it is so. He is the One who said He would never leave nor forsake you. "And surely I am with you always, to the very end of the age" (Matt. 28:20).

Adapted from *The First Four Years are the Hardest* (InterVarsity Press, 1980) by Michael Pountney.

3

Not Thirsty, Still Hungry

Why you should consider a short term

by Steven C. Hawthorne

Steven C. Hawthorne has led several short-term teams in Asia and the Middle East. Truths in this article were discovered during a team Bible study while on a short term in a Muslim city.

Who started the short-term mission craze? It might have been Jesus Himself. He used short expeditions to train His followers. He sent 12 disciples for a few weeks to visit villages in Galilee. Later, He sent 70 others to do the same thing.

You couldn't really call these expeditions "missions" in the sense that we use the word today. They went to their own kind of people. They spoke the same language and lived with the same customs. There was nothing cross-cultural about it.

But on one occasion, Jesus took them deep into a foreign culture. What His disciples learned during those few days is essentially what Jesus teaches people today during cross-cultural short terms. The story is told in chapter four of John's Gospel.

The disciples were trekking from Jerusalem to Galilee. They used a shortcut through Samaria to make the trip in one day. About noon, they stopped at a well near one of the towns. The disciples hurried into town for "Mac-Bagels" or something else quick to eat.

Jesus stayed at the well and talked to a lady who was getting a jar of water. He asked her for a drink. She was shocked. In that culture, men didn't talk with women. Even more amazing was the fact that a Jew had spoken to a Samaritan. Samaritans were considered religiously "icky" by Jews. They were part Jew and part Gentile. Jews usually never spoke with them. And Jews certainly never ate or drank with Samaritans. Asking for a drink of water was a fairly radical thing to do.

When the disciples returned, they succeeded in scaring off the lady and began eating lunch in a hurry. They had to make Galilee by sundown.

But Jesus surprised them by not eating a bite. Instead He said,
"I have food to eat that you know nothing about." That comment
really set off a discussion. Did He have a secret supply? Had the
Samaritan lady given Him something to eat? Had Jesus been
breaking bread miraculously again?

None of the above: "'My food,' said Jesus, 'is to do the will of
him who sent me and to finish his work'" (verse 34).

What did Jesus mean? They had been doing God's work. They
were doing evangelism. They were making disciples. They were
even starting to out-baptize John the Baptist (verses 1, 2). What
more did they need to know about doing God's work?

They needed to know that God wanted them to serve Him with
a view to finishing the work of the Gospel. They weren't going at
it as if there were a larger purpose which must be finished. They
were merely doing good work for God.

So Jesus told them to lift up their eyes. We don't know for sure,
but it is possible that they looked up and saw the same Samaritan
lady coming back, this time with several leading men from the
town (verse 30). There were probably six men in particular who
were interested in someone who knew every scandalous event in
this woman's life (verses 18, 29).

The disciples had just ignored the people around them in the
Samaritan town, thinking they were just a source of a snack for the
road. Jesus wanted to change their perspective. These people mat-
tered. Right then, not later. The new perspective was that every
people group was to be touched significantly. God's purpose
wasn't complete until the Gospel was proclaimed fruitfully among
every people—even Samaritans.

Not Thirsty, Still Hungry

What Jesus wanted the disciples to see that day, He also wants
us to see today. Somebody has to actually go across borders and
social boundaries to bring the Gospel to people without a witness.
Why go on a short-term mission? For the same reason Jesus took
these guys to touch some Samaritans: to finish the work that the
Father sent us to do. The Father is seeking true worshipers (verse
23). And apparently He wants them from every people (Matt.
28:18-20; Rev. 7:9).

If you go at all, even for a summer, go to get more true worshipers of God. Don't go into missions to just get a few more people on
your side. The rest of the world views missions as just so much
religious sport—the Christians win a few and the Muslims win a

few, or the Baptists gain while the Catholics lose.

If this is all that world evangelization means to you, you might get tired of it soon. You stand a good chance of becoming secretly cynical about missions and dropping out of serving God altogether.

Most Christians have tasted the living water Jesus offered the woman (verse 14). They are no longer thirsty. God has satisfied the longing for eternal life. Life becomes a well "springing up to eternal life."

But some Christians are like the disciples—still hungry, but for what they do not know. It seems there has to be something more than dry church programs, family devotions, and being good. Perhaps discipleship makes sense only while living with the life purpose of Jesus. He said that this purpose was as much a part of His life as the food He ate. He had given Himself fully to completing God's purpose in the world, and it was a feast of destiny, significance, meaning, and joy.

A Change in Perspective

But Jesus knew that they wouldn't ever start eating that "food" unless they tasted the realities of bringing the Gospel to a people who had not yet heard. That's why He got them involved pretty heavily in Samaritan culture for a few days (verse 40).

Before Jesus got them working in Samaritan culture, He put two common proverbs in their minds so that they could make sense out of their short term. Keep them in your mind. They'll help you start in and keep going.

The first is,"...four months more and then the harvest..." (verse 35). This proverb was commonly used among grain farmers who really couldn't do much but wait for rain after they sowed their seed. Irrigation wasn't an option. They depended on rain. Weeding wasn't practical. There wasn't much to do but wait until the right time. We would say something like, "Everything in its time."

No doubt they believed that God would eventually do something for the Gentiles and the Samaritans. But the disciples assumed that it wasn't really the right time to do anything about all these non-Jews. Jesus challenged them to look again: "Open your eyes and look at the fields! They are ripe for harvest." The disciples had seen these very people only as storekeepers from whom they could buy bread. Jesus wanted them to see those same people as a harvest for God.

A short term will change your perspective on the world. On a short term, you can sense the urgent need of real people. Statistics become people with names. But you can also see how God is touching those very people. You can see how even you can make a difference in meeting significant needs. Perhaps there is no better way to see the world as Jesus sees it but to interrupt your routine and serve overseas for a short time.

A Challenge of Partnership

"One sows and another reaps" (verses 36-38). People often muttered this second proverb when they felt that life was futile; why work hard? Someone else will get the good and glory for all the hard effort. Jesus affirmed the proverb, but in the opposite sense: your life and labor amount to something significant, but only as you team up with others.

The disciples were watching Jesus reap the fruit sown by prophets centuries earlier. These men of God had so sensitized the entire town with the expectancy that one day God would do something great through a Messiah (verse 25) that almost the entire town eagerly trusted Him. The disciples had "entered into the labor" of others (verse 38, NASB) by finishing what other servants of God had begun long before.

Getting the world evangelized is obviously bigger than any of us. You'll probably step into someone else's ministry if you go on a short term. A short term is a great way to discover how valuable and yet how dependent you really are. Jesus said that the sower and reaper can rejoice together. Don't miss out on the joy of partnership.

The task is so great that God has used every generation of His people since Abraham to complete His purpose. You're stepping into something just as ancient as it is urgent. Whether God guides you to return home or to stay overseas for the rest of your life, a short term can help you sort out your role in it all.

Jesus: Savior of the World

You might discover something fresh about Jesus during a short term. The disciples hadn't seen it before their cross-cultural experience. But the Samaritans discovered who Jesus really was: "the Savior of the world" (verse 42). If He's nothing more than a "personal savior" to you, then you might gain a lot from a short-term mission. You might come to know a world-sized God offering you a world-sized part in His plan. Live for a purpose larger than yourself. It's like food you can eat. If you're hungry for life purpose, bite into world evangelization.

Motive Mix

Why am I going?

You'll be better off if you try to sort out the reasons and motives prompting you to go. Almost any missionary, short-term or "lifer," is going to have a variety of motives. Some are pure and spiritual. Others are admittedly personal. That's okay. It's probably healthy to have a blend of motives. Whatever you do, examine them. If you don't, you may find yourself unready for hardships and challenges you didn't expect.

Below is a list of reasons why many people go on a short-term mission. Read through the entire list and mark ten items which reflect most closely your hopes and desires. Then return to those ten items and assign each one a numerical value:

> *3 = most powerful motivator*
> *2 = strong motivator*
> *1 = not so strong a motivator*

I want to go on a short term...

Personal:
_____ for the excitement and fun of travel.
_____ to see if I want to be a missionary.
_____ to experience another culture.
_____ to get away from home.
_____ to get experience in a certain skill.
_____ to get training as a Christian worker.
_____ to buy duty-free electronics.
_____ to add to my list of countries visited.
_____ to see and experience real poverty.
_____ as a way to spend a summer growing.
_____ to find a mate with interests like mine.
_____ other: _____

Spiritual:
_____ to know God as never before.
_____ to show God that I'm serious about following Him.
_____ because I have a missionary call.
_____ because God has told me specifically to go.
_____ to gain favor with God.
_____ to use my gifts for God.
_____ other: _____

External:

_____ because my friends are going.

_____ because someone I trust has urged me to go.

_____ because I'm being pressured to do it.

_____ to get my missions duty over with.

_____ other: _____

Cause-related:

_____ to help finish the task of world evangelization.

_____ to better mobilize my church.

_____ to help establish God's kingdom.

_____ because it's strategic to help nations.

_____ to help rebuild a world with God's justice.

_____ because Jesus commands it of us all.

_____ other: _____

Needs-related:

_____ to help hungry children.

_____ to give overworked missionaries a break.

_____ because people are going to hell without the Gospel.

_____ because of compassion for poverty-stricken people.

_____ other: _____

Now, within each of the five categories, add up the numbers that you have assigned to the ten most important motivating factors you have selected. There are no "correct" answers. You may have 15 or 20 points in a category, or none at all. The important thing is to recognize your motives and to work on balancing your reasons for going. There really is no "ideal" or "correct" balance of motives.

You shouldn't necessarily be disappointed with your motives. It may be better to do the "right" thing for the "wrong" motives than to do nothing at all. Whatever you do, be honest with yourself. Talk things over with a friend. And talk things over with God.

Get Set

Where in the world should you go? And which opportunity is the right one for you? You can't go it alone, and you shouldn't try to make the decisions alone. Get set for your short term with help from the right people.

4

Opening the World

**A look at the length and
breadth of worldwide opportunities**

by Dick Staub

Dick Staub is host of ChicagoTalks, a daily talk show on WYLL-FM in Chicago.

With so many thousands of opportunities to serve overseas, I can almost guarantee there's an overseas short-term mission opportunity that fits you. In fact, I believe that almost anybody with two weeks to two years of time who desires to serve God overseas can do just that, regardless of how aged or unskilled he or she may feel. Here's an overview of the opportunities.

Go With Your Church

Talk to your pastor or missions committee leader (or missions pastor, if your church has one). Ask them if your church is planning to send a short-term mission team. If they aren't, perhaps your inquiry will spur them on to form one.

Ask for the address of your denomination's mission agency. Many of these now offer short terms of service. Costs and locations will vary, but the options increase every year.

Go With a Mission Agency

There are literally scores of mission agencies (sometimes called mission boards) that accept short-termers. On a short-term mission with an agency, you have the advantage of experienced leadership, training, and a community of people to talk to before, during, and after your trip. Most of these agencies require you to raise the needed finances for your trip. This, however, doesn't present an insurmountable barrier at all; tens of thousands of short-termers manage to raise their own financial support every year.

The range of skills used for short terms may surprise you. I have discovered a need for vocations including auditors, nurses, English teachers, elementary and secondary teachers (many subject), ophthalmologists, maintenance workers, business managers, dorm parents, office workers, builders, X-ray technicians, bookkeepers, radio engineers, translators, typists, agricultural advisers, biomedical equipment technicians, dentists, camp managers, language teachers, basketball players, mechanics, artists, food service managers, community development advisers, computer programmers, maritime workers, cooks, musicians, plumbers, nutritionists, librarians, and, well, you get the idea.

Whatever you can do, God can use it, even if you've used the skill only as a hobby or in a summer job. You could end up leading small group Bible studies; building a road, a clinic, or a church building; dispensing medical supplies; communicating the Gospel through friendships as part of an evangelism team; handing out literature; teaching guitar; running a warehouse; giving hugs to handicapped children; or just spreading the love of God wherever you go.

What are these mission agencies like? Each has a distinct personality because it's composed of unique people. Some have been around for decades. Some are brand new. Some specialize in one particular kind of work (drilling wells, for example) or one particular area of the world. Others do everything from church planting to reforestation. Some require a graduate degree even for their short-term programs; others take almost any sincere, growing Christian.

Some offer months of training, others only hours. For some agencies, short-termers function as an integral part of the evangelistic goals of the mission; for others, short-termers serve as support workers who answer phones, build clinics, or repair cars so that church planters and doctors can serve more effectively.

Connecting With an Agency

For a more specific list of opportunities that match your skills and geographic interests, use Intercristo's Christian Placement Network. This service is well worth the nominal fee for processing a simple profile of your skills and interests with thousands of opportunities. Call 1-800-426-1342, or write Intercristo (19303 Fremont Ave. N., Seattle, WA 98133).

Write the Interdenominational Foreign Mission Association (IFMA, P.O. Box 398, Wheaton, IL 60189-0398) for a current list of opportunities (many career-length) from different agencies.

Contact the Evangelical Fellowship of Mission Agencies (EFMA, 1023 15th St. NW, Washington, DC 20005; Ph. 202-789-1011, Fax 202-843-0392) about mission organizations offering short-terms.

Put yourself in InterVarsity's Mission Placement Service. This free service, sometimes called "the fishpond," puts dozens of mission agencies with hundreds of opportunities directly in touch with you to present opportunities which would best mesh with your skills and desires. It's open to those who are firmly committed to going overseas, or who at least feel it's probable that they might serve overseas for at least a year. Write to InterVarsity Missions, P.O. Box 7895, Madison, WI 53707-7895 or call 1-800-DECLARE.

Go as a Student

For college students, spending a summer or entire year (or longer) studying in a foreign school can be an ideal way to combine education with ministry. Also, students can often enter countries closed to traditional missionary activity.

Regardless of your area of interest, you can study overseas. You can study archeology on digs in Israel, medieval history in ancient castles in France, Asian cultures in the Himalayas, art in Beijing, social work in Honduras, even Russian language at Moscow University. Costs vary—some schools are very expensive, some surprisingly affordable—and grants and work-study options abound. Not all colleges have complete information on overseas study opportunities. Contact a large university with a good reputation in your area of interest.

Studying Abroad

Checking out schooling overseas can be easier than you think, if you have some help.

Global Opportunities helps Christians find study opportunities abroad and offers counsel on how to be an effective witness while studying. Contact them at 1600 Elizabeth St., Pasadena, CA 91104 or call (818) 797-3233.

One secular resource is the Institute for International Education (205 E. 42nd St., New York, NY 10017). They're a gold mine of data on study programs and grants worldwide.

Go as a Tentmaker

A tentmaker, a person who practices self-support like the apostle Paul, engages in ministry while working at a paid secular job. Opportunities for such work, even for short periods, abound. In many places, there's no way to get in a country except through a secular job. In some situations, there's no better way to get within "witnessing range" of people than to work right beside them.

Although the expense is often minimal, the cost may be high.

Your witness may be restricted, and you may even be isolated from fellow Christians. As a prospective tentmaker, consider your ability to carry out ministry alone or in situations hostile to the Gospel. Check into the possibility of forming a support group in your home church, going with a team of tentmakers, or hooking up with a mission agency or local church in the area to which you're going. It doesn't have to be an "either/or" decision with many mission agencies; you can be a tentmaker and an affiliate of some mission agencies.

Consider the Peace Corps, which offers good cross-cultural exposure. Although your freedom to witness is restricted, it offers more ministry opportunity than you might have believed.

If you speak decent American English, you can almost write your ticket as a teacher of conversational English to students or business people, sometimes even with minimal training. From China to Egypt and from Morocco to Japan, English teachers are needed. Often the best approach is to put out feelers indicating that you're available, and things will begin to happen.

I could go on about ways to live, witness, and serve in a short term abroad. Americans have sold popcorn (a novelty in many countries), told stories in Russia, led children's activities among Palestinian refugees, and dug freshwater canals in work camps in Turkey. Your imagination could be the only limit

Tentmaking Opportunities

Global Resources publishes the *International Employment Gazette*, a 32-page biweekly tabloid newspaper with more than 400 overseas job openings per issue. Also available is the International Placement Network, which provides job openings based on an individual's occupation and geographic interests. Contact Global Resources at (803) 235-4444, or write to 1525 Wade Hampton Blvd., Greenville, SC 29609.

Global Opportunities helps Christians link their marketable skills with jobs all over the world. They offer computerized job matching with personal counseling, pre-field orientation, and liaison with Christians overseas. Contact Global Opportunities, 1600 Elizabeth St., Pasadena, CA 91104, (818) 797-3233.

Let's Go

One of my most significant learning experiences in college was a summer spent in Indonesia. There I saw a third-world culture, engaged in missions work, and probably most importantly, began a lifelong process of trying to be a better steward of the resources

God invested in me.

Don't let this chance pass you by. It's so easy to get bogged down with all the trappings of the American success fantasy and never quite get around to exposing yourself to challenges faced by Christians in countries where Christian faith doesn't come as cheaply. I urge you to consider short-term service abroad in the name of Jesus. Christians with daring and imagination now have unparalleled opportunities to make an impact for Christ.

Who gets overseas? Those who are determined, who knock on every overseas door, and—even if finding them hard to open—keep knocking.

What to Ask an Agency

Every agency is different, and every opportunity that an agency offers is unique. Use the chart below to learn about each agency or opportunity that interests you.

Make your evaluations in pencil. After comparing a few opportunities, you may change your mind about what is best for you. Make copies of this blank form and use it to learn about several opportunities.

Even if you're considering going without attachment to a mission agency, such as in a tentmaking capacity, ask yourself the same questions.

Name of Agency: _____

	Yes	Okay	No
Length of stay: _____	___	___	___
Type of work: _____	___	___	___
Amount of work: _____	___	___	___
Location: _____	___	___	___
Training: _____	___	___	___
in support raising: _____	___	___	___
in the culture: _____	___	___	___
in teamwork: _____	___	___	___
debriefing: _____	___	___	___
Contact with other culture: _____	___	___	___
Cost: _____	___	___	___
Team atmosphere: _____	___	___	___
Doctrine: _____	___	___	___
Living environment: _____	___	___	___
Leadership, authority structure: _____	___	___	___
Potential for career: _____	___	___	___
Others' counsel about it: _____	___	___	___

5

Discovering the Best Short-Term Mission

How to decide which one is best for you

by Steven C. Hawthorne

Steven C. Hawthorne has led short-term teams in Asia and the Middle East. He presently serves with Antioch Network, an organization serving churches sending teams to unreached peoples.

You have an "overchoice" problem in missions. Hundreds of mission agencies have opportunities. Many of them want you or someone like you. Yet each is different. Which one is right for you? Which one will best fulfill God's call on your life?

I remember the strange mixture of exhilaration and despair that I felt at Urbana '76. I was open to missions, but I was paralyzed by the overchoice. I spent hours studying a list of mission opportunities available at that conference. I let my eye pass over a listing if I didn't like the name of the organization or if I didn't care for the city in which the headquarters was located. It occurred to me then that I didn't know anything significant about the missions I was rejecting.

My mind was bouncing back and forth: Did I want to go for a summer or leave for a whole year? Did I want to go to Africa or work in India? How about using my major? Should I be willing to do construction work, or would that be a waste of time? Evangelism opportunities were all over the place, but at that time I was needlessly suspicious of literature evangelism, so I skipped over many "street evangelism" opportunities.

I knew that I was being arbitrary. I also began to realize there was no way I was going to get a master's degree in mission opportunities in one afternoon. So, not wanting to quit the job I had lined up for the following summer, I made the very bold decision to stay home. Somehow, God eventually got me overseas, despite my confusion.

What I wanted was a simple list of steps. I might as well have waited for a yellow brick road to appear to lead me to the Emerald City of Oz. There just isn't any simplistic sequence of things to do. Lives like yours and mine aren't easily squeezed into a hopscotch game of one step followed by another.

Instead, I've learned to take note of six decision areas which need to come together. Everyone works through them in a different order and in a unique way.

You might come to the process with some assumptions in one or two areas, but everybody decides or defaults at each of these points. Face them all. Identify your assumptions. Choose which areas should be priority as you sense God's guidance. Develop criteria for deciding which options fit your situation in each area. Pray through them all. Get counsel from others.

The sequence in which you consider each area makes a difference. For example, one who assumes he or she will go overseas for the summer (term) to play basketball (talent) with a sports ministry (team) may not be able to choose between going to Mexico City or to Muslims in Indonesia (target).

Target

Consider your target. What need will you touch? To which country will you go? What people? Which city?

For some people, targeting is the main event. Perhaps they feel that God has "called" them to a particular country. Others figure it is important to go where they are most needed. Others have learned to put their finger on places and peoples which are strategic in light of the big picture of world evangelization.

For example, some people set their heart on going to Kenya, and all their choices follow from that. Perhaps you have known people who eat and sleep China. When they look for a short-term opportunity, they will look first for chances to go to China.

Task

Consider your task. What kind of activity will you be doing from day to day? What goals will you accomplish?

Some short-termers are open to serve in just about any way. Others start out fixed on a particular job description. You may have your heart set on digging wells, church planting, nursing, literacy work, helping in churches, playing with orphans, street evangelism, or even building runways in the jungle. Get acquainted with the range of fascinating possibilities. Dream boldly, but beware of spinning scenarios in your mind which are out of reach during the short time you'll stay.

Team

Consider your team. With whom will you go? Which mission agency? What relationship will you have with national churches? With your home church?

To step into a short term usually means that a team is taking you on. Suddenly, you will be involved in something larger than yourself or your own career. It's really a matter of trust. Mission agencies will probably accept you, believing that you will contribute to the task God has given them. You need to trust the leadership of that agency to help guide your service. If you choose your team first, then that agency will usually be heavily involved in determining your target, task, and term.

Carefully consider several agencies. Don't get stuck on one mission just because you know someone who went out with them or because you have supported them in the past. Develop some criteria and go shopping.

A large part of your total team is the church which is sending you. Don't leave them out of your decision at any point.

Talents

Consider your talents, gifts, and strengths. What spiritual gifts are called for? What do you like to do most? What weaknesses do you have?

Many people start here on the search. There may be something they are good at, like basketball or playing guitar. Some are pleasantly surprised that their special gift can be put to use in missions. Others get trapped by their gifts and put undue expectations on mission leadership to assign them to duties in areas in which they excel or have interests. They can easily find themselves disappointed and resentful when given tasks which don't give them that magic feeling of "self-fulfillment." Don't get involved in missions, even for a short term, if you merely seek to feel fulfilled and good about yourself. Mission work is work. It's fundamentally service.

On the other hand, try to find something that fits you best. You may not feel like you have much to offer. You do. You may not feel like you have too many well-developed expectations of your time. Silent expectations are the most dangerous. Get in touch with them.

Training

Consider your training. What are you prepared to do? What can you be ready for?

You may begin the selection process by examining your education, experience, and qualifications. This is a worthy consideration, but sometimes a poor place to start. Although you might find something which fits you, you'll probably miss several key opportunities. It's odd how Americans assume that people should do something in the field of their college major, when most of us do work in areas entirely unrelated to it.

Be sure to inventory all of your qualifications. You may be more prepared than you think. Check to see if different mission structures offer training as part of the short-term experience.

Term

Consider your term of service. What length commitment will you be making? Are you thinking of just spending a summer, a semester, or a year? Do you want an option to extend your short term longer? Are you seriously exploring how to spend most of your life overseas if this short term works out well?

Consider how much more you may gain and give if you commit yourself for a year. Be wise about severing ties and quitting jobs, but short-term missions is missions, after all. Expect to give up something in order to give something. Beware of trying to work missions into your schedule when it seems convenient. It's rarely convenient to change the world.

Putting It All Together

Here are five ways to sort through your options:

1. Find a friend to help you. People don't do radical things by themselves. And face it, you are doing something radical by going overseas. Find a trusted friend or leader in your church who will understand your motives and mission hopes.

2. Stretch out your future on a time line. This is one way to identify the roadblocks and the conflicting agendas. A well-thought-through time line will show where you are attempting a "mission impossible" with utterly unrealistic expectations.

3. Stretch your faith. On the other hand, don't settle for what is merely possible. God may lead you beyond the easy or the obvious. You'll have to trust Him no matter where you go, but prepare yourself for some risk-taking ventures.

4. Face your fears. You may have good cause to worry. Maybe you have a phobia about getting shots. Perhaps you fear being single the rest of your life. Or you might fail miserably and be embarrassed before everyone who supported you. If you dredge up all the fears and look at them in the light, though some will still be scary, you may get a laugh out of some silly scenarios in your mind. This exercise may not make you feel any more courageous, but you won't be paralyzed with wrong impressions.

5. Deal with freedoms. You may have to give up some of the prerogatives you think are yours in order to be truly free to choose the right mission opportunity. Obey God. It's not a matter of finding something that "fits" you or furthers your career. The real issue is being utterly mastered by Christ. You may need to face up to a mistaken sense of entitlement. Do you somehow believe that God is rigging up the whole world to revolve around your own self-fulfillment? Be prepared to relinquish areas of your future or dreams you thought were yours to decide. If you let them go into God's hand, He has promised to give you more than you bargained for. "Whoever wants to save his life will lose it, but whoever loses his life for me and for the gospel will save it" (Mark 8:35). Jim Elliot said it this way: "He is no fool who gives up what he cannot keep to gain what he cannot lose."

CHECKPOINT

Decision Points

Use these statements to find out how you've already begun to decide which opportunity might be right for you. How firm you are in some areas will influence your decisions in other areas.

Read through the entire list and check statements that reflect most closely your hopes and desires. Then return to those statements and decide how certain you are about each.

	Certain	Some Idea	Unsure
Target (the people, city, or country I'll touch):			
__ I want to work with a certain people or kind of people.			
__ I already have a particular country or city in mind.			
__ I want to avoid certain places or kinds of people.			
Task (the kind of work I'll do):			
__ I hope to do outreach/evangelistic activities.			
__ I want to focus my time on the needs of churches.			
__ I want to be involved with physical and social needs.			
Team (the organization I'll go with):			
__ I want to link up with my church or denomination.			
__ I'm leaning toward one mission agency already.			
__ I know with what kind of organizations I want to go.			
Talents (the skills and gifts I'll use):			
__ It's important to use my special skills and experience.			
__ The job has to mesh with my known spiritual gifts.			
__ I want to do things that I haven't done before.			
Training (the schooling I have or need):			
__ I want further training as part of the short term.			
__ I have professional training which *could* be used.			
__ I want to do something that won't freeze my career.			
Term (the length of time I'll be gone):			
__ I just have the summer.			
__ I want something with long-term options.			
__ I have to set a limit on the length of time.			

In which of the six areas (Target, Task, Team, Talents, Training, Term) do you have the most certainty? The least? Rank your certainties in the order of how strongly you want each of them to influence your decision regarding your short term. In which areas could you use a little more flexibility? In which areas should you probably be more decisive?

6

Make the Right Connections

How to involve others
in the venture from the very start

by Lucinda Secrest McDowell

Lucinda Secrest McDowell is a writer and speaker from Wethersfield, Connecticut. A former missions pastor, she has trained short-term missionaries and produced a daily radio news program, "Christians Around the World."

Now it's happening to you. You never thought it would. You've watched other apparently normal people go overseas for years. They come back in decent shape, but different. You've always looked on career missionaries with awe, but you could never identify with them. As you watched others commit big chunks of their lives to cross-cultural ministry, your prayers might have been, "Here am I, Lord, send them!"

But now you're seriously considering giving it a try, perhaps for just a summer. You almost don't want to tell anybody. What if you don't go through with it? Should you keep your plans under wraps until you leave?

Tell somebody what you are thinking. In fact, tell several people early on while you are still mulling it over. There's no spiritual "Charles Lindbergh" award for attempting solo trips overseas with no guidance and coaching from others.

Some people have the opposite problem. Far from feeling like they want to prove something by doing great exploits on their own, they want to break away from the pressure of expectations of friends and family. A short-term experience may appear as a chance to break away, to get far away from home, school, or job, and serve the Lord with abandon. You might be tempted to "disconnect" from the world you've known.

Don't disconnect. Don't pull off a covert operation. More than ever, you're going to need the wisdom and backing of godly people. Some of those people you will have known for some time. Some will be new to you. But if you want to have any kind of success, pursue relationships with key people, especially while you are considering where to go and how to get there.

You'll need to connect with others in three ways before you leave: receive *counsel* from trusted friends and family, *consult* with key leaders in mission structures and in your church, and *communicate* with interested friends and supporters.

Counsel

The primary connection you need to make is with God through serious prayer. Make it "open heart" prayer. Come to the Lord in total honesty, with all of your hopes, plans, and fears. Verbalize each one specifically as an act of trust. Give them over to the Lord, expecting His answers to come. To "pray through" an issue or situation like this is not a mere devotional exercise; it requires commitment and discipline. That's why it's unlikely that you'll get very far praying by yourself.

Seek out a prayer partner (of the same sex). Covenant with them to seek God's will together concerning every aspect of this short-term mission venture. Don't forget to be still and listen for God's answers as they come, often in unexpected ways.

Hopefully, you are already part of a small group of Christians who meet regularly for Bible study, prayer, and fellowship. If not, pray that God will give you time with some friends to whom you can be committed, people who share a global vision and a dedication to Christ. You may have to organize gatherings. You may have to make appointments or travel a distance to see these people. Do whatever it takes to get like-minded Christians to join you in exploring your heart and the opportunities that God gives you.

The crucial phase of exploring opportunities shouldn't be done alone. Dr. Robert Munger says, "Jesus called His disciples to a committed company. We must not presume to be solitary followers of Jesus Christ. Seek the counsel of trusted believers. To move out step by step alongside our Lord with bright faith and a warm heart, we need one another as fellow followers—praying for one another and supporting one another."

Within the sphere of this community relationship, ask yourself some hard questions. "How solid is my commitment to Christ? What gifts do I have to offer for service? Are my reasons for pursuing short-term missions healthy and appropriate?" Discuss various mission opportunities and consider together which ones may fit you best at this time. Together you'll be able to see the pitfalls and some of the astounding possibilities.

Consult

Seek out more mature Christians who can give you solid wisdom and fresh information about your short-term mission dreams. Start with your pastor. Keep him informed early on of your thinking. Ask for his advice and his recommendation of other leaders in the local church who might be able to give you even more counsel. Some churches are fortunate enough to have a special pastor with missions responsibilities. Find out which leader in your congregation or denomination leads the missions concerns of your church.

If you are a student, you may have a college chaplain. Leaders of campus ministries such as Navigators, Campus Crusade, and InterVarsity usually offer sound insights. Often they have seen your "track record" in ministry and spiritual growth.

Open up with your family. Before the process goes too far, arrange a time to discuss your vision and hopes with significant people in your family, especially your parents. Plan ahead so that you can discuss your dreams and plans in a personal encounter, not through a letter or telephone call. It is best to give some background about your thinking and growing process as a Christian concerned for the world.

Many non-Christian parents may respond in shock based on their concept of missions and missionaries. Your most crucial task will be to share with them the "why" behind your desire to serve overseas. Without a trace of condescension, fill the role of interpreter of how God is working in the world through people today.

You may hear protests like, "Is *this* why I paid for you to get a computer science degree?" or "No daughter of mine is going begging for money!" Other parents, whatever their Christian persuasion, may fear your proposed living and working conditions.

There is no simple formula for handling the myriad of responses from your family, but try to anticipate their concerns. Calmly and non-defensively give them as much information as possible. Listen carefully to what they have to say.

In his book *Life and Work on the Mission Field* (Baker, 1980), missions professor J. Herbert Kane addresses this issue: "Nowhere does the Bible suggest that parents, Christian or non-Christian, have the right to come between their children and the will of God. From a purely humanistic point of view, it is wrong for parents to force their plans on their children. It is doubly wrong when these plans run contrary to the will of God." *[Note: You may want to review the article "Honoring Parents" by Dr. David M. Howard on page 67.]*

Talk with mission representatives. You may have to talk over the phone, but get to know mission representatives. Most are well-informed and willing to coach you through fears and concerns.

Meet missionaries. Once the location is set, do whatever you can to meet former missionaries from that country or other short-termers who have preceded you. Often these people rate as "experts" on where you're going, and they're usually very pleased to share about the life and culture you can expect.

Communicate

Tell people what you plan to do as soon as you come to a clear decision about your direction. Keep a list of those you want to keep informed. You will probably need to give these people updates a few times before you go. Don't forget to thank those who are giving you prayer and/or financial support.

Make connections with your local church, meeting first with your pastor. Your church may even have a missions committee. Obviously, check in with that group. Try to arrange a time to present your expectations and prayer requests. Promise to keep them informed through regular prayer letters. Express a desire to be formally commissioned at a morning or an evening service so that you can feel truly "sent out" from your church home.

You may have a pastor or a leader who does not enthusiastically embrace your plans for short-term missions. Be prepared to accept less support than you would have desired, and ask the Lord to use you in this situation as a possible catalyst to bring about a new attitude toward missions in that church.

The communication process takes time. It can make you feel vulnerable. You may feel rejected by those who misunderstand. But one thing you can count on: God is with you through it all.

And what does God do? In his book *The First Four Years are the Hardest* (InterVarsity Press, 1980), Michael Pountney reminds us of God's faithfulness: "As you bring to the top of your list the genuine desire to get involved in adventurous faith, God smiles to Himself, and brings out His gifts. Because as you commit yourself to Him, He commits Himself to you and equips you for the job. And He will not be your debtor; He will unload on you some of the marvels and glories and pains of His kingdom. Watch out—it might hurt. But you will love it, and you will grow."

7

How to Talk With Mission People

Entering the agency universe

by Gail C. Bennett

Gail C. Bennett writes and edits the Overseas Council Newsletter of the Overseas Council for Theological Education and Missions.

Linking up with a mission agency to go overseas may seem like a lot of unnecessary red tape. Captain Kirk's spellbinding voice saying "to boldly go where no man has gone before" rings in our ears. Lost and needy people wait to be reached. Let's not wait around, folks, let's *move*.

That's a good idea, but it's just not as easy as it sounds. Even the heroic crew of the *Enterprise* took directives for each starship mission from Federation headquarters. A mission agency has a vital role to play in sending you forth on a short-term expedition.

The problem you will quickly discover, however, is that there are a plethora of mission agencies, and not just any agency will do for you. Mission agencies differ vastly in their theologies, ministry philosophies, goals and objectives, and the environments in which they work. Denominational agencies often limit their candidates to members from their congregations.

Some agencies organize structured, carefully tailored programs for short-term missionaries. Others nearly leave short-termers to fend for themselves. Some agencies are short-term specialists. Others send out no short-term missionaries. Your mission task is to sort through the tangle of possibilities and hook up with an agency that meets your needs, goals, and aspirations.

When you take the plunge and contact mission agency people, however, you may feel as if you've accidentally hit the "warp drive" button and passed into another universe. This was my experience. The vocabulary they used couldn't be found in my version of *Webster's dictionary*. And they were so preoccupied with missions. Despite my growing interest, I felt threatened by their all-encompassing enthusiasm. It struck me as judgmental.

Instead of finding creatures from a foreign galaxy, though, I soon discovered that mission agency people were a lot like me. And when I knew my objectives, knew the ropes, and knew myself better, communicating with them became a lot easier.

Know Your Questions

Mission agencies with short-term programs want to locate suitable personnel as much as you want to find an appropriate agency. They could spend hours describing their agency while you check off the pluses and minuses as you hear them. But you'll both be happier if you know what you want from a short-term program and a mission agency before you begin serious dialogue. Develop some clear, well-thought-through questions that are of importance to you. These can be drawn from the following four areas.

1. Theology. What's their view of God, man, the Church, and missions? Are there theological distinctives that set them apart from other ministries? Do they cooperate with those who hold other positions? How do you feel about their answers?

2. Ministry philosophy. What's their emphasis: evangelism, nurture, or service? Does their approach to ministry emphasize flexibility and spontaneity, or stability and structured objectives? Are they people-oriented (evangelizing, nurturing, or serving people through a variety of programs) or task-oriented (specialists in radio broadcasting, literature production, etc.)? How do they view the roles of men and women in ministry? Could you see yourself fitting into an agency with their philosophy?

3. Goals and objectives. What will they have you do? How do they expect you to benefit? What role will they play in helping you develop prayer and financial support? How does it all correspond with your own goals and objectives? Or perhaps a better question: Are the goals of this mission worthy of setting aside some of your own goals?

4. Ministry environment. In what countries do they place short-term missionaries? Would you work in English, or would you need a second language? Do they work with people culturally similar to you, or very different? What living standards are expected of their short-term missionaries? Will you be in partnership with other short-term missionaries, professional missionaries, or both? Is this the environment you want?

Know the Ropes

"They *won't* want me to take a personality test, will they?" wailed the anxious prospective short-term worker. "I get brain cramps when I take tests. They'll think I'm suicidal." In fact, most short-termers aren't asked to take temperament analysis tests. But his anxious cry betrays a normal fear of the unknown. "What do I have to do," he is asking, "before I can get underway?" Serious dialogue with a mission agency usually involves four basic points of contact.

1. Instigation. This occurs when you express interest in a particular short-term program. Often, short-term workers get exposed to an agency by friends who served previously. Other contacts come through recommendations from church leaders, literature, and conferences.

In most cases you'll write the agency (address it to the personnel director or director of short-term programs), indicating your particular interest and asking for more information. They'll usually send you informational brochures and an appropriate application form. If some of your questions (see "Know Your Questions" on page 52) aren't answered by materials they send you, write again and ask those questions specifically. You may initiate contact with several agencies before selecting one to which you will apply.

2. Application. Application procedures range from simple to elaborate. You'll probably be asked general questions about yourself, your conversion and spiritual pilgrimage, and your interest in short-term missions. You could receive medical forms along with the application, or a medical exam may be required later. You may be asked to supply the names of two or more references (usually a church elder, pastor, or Christian leader who knows you well). Instead, you could be supplied with reference forms for you to distribute. (The agency has a vested interest in knowing if your church is behind you and if it will support you with prayer and money.)

3. Evaluation. Each agency has its own system for evaluating prospective applicants. Operation Mobilisation, for example, runs short summer campaigns and one- and two-year short-term programs. If you're interested in a one- or two-year program, your application will be reviewed, and you'll have an interview with someone from the home office. If you both sense a green light at the end of the interview, you'll be asked to attend a one-week orientation and participate in a month-long summer campaign. After this, you will have another interview with someone from the home office and a separate interview with field personnel to mutually agree on a suitable field service. Besides giving opportunity for evaluation, these experiences provide the added plus of good training.

4. Assignment. After approval, you will receive your field assignment and need to raise remaining support. You can expect to receive travel information and other details (such as the immunizations you'll need) closer to the date of your departure.

Know Yourself

Most of us, on occasion, fall prey to one of two traps: pride or insecurity. Either can derail you along the way in your effort to find an appropriate agency.

Suppose, for example, you run into an unimpressive mission agency representative wearing yesterday's suit, sporting a ragged crew cut, and using out-of-date missions terminology. Try not to judge him too quickly.

A missionary who worked in a remote jungle received an alumni survey in the mail from his former university. The survey was designed to uncover the prestige level of the school's graduates. The first question was, "Do you own your own home?" Looking out the unclad window of the grass shack in which he lived, he answered, "Yes, I own my own home." The next question asked, "Do you own a boat?" His eye caught sight of the log-hewn canoe he used to travel up the river. "Yes," he answered, "I own a boat." The next question was, "Will you be traveling abroad this year?" Since he planned to return home on furlough soon, again he answered, "yes." Finally, the survey posed a list of salary options, for him to check. Scanning the options he drew another box beneath the lowest one and checked it. Then with a smile on his face, he mailed it back.

Real consequence, as he knew, is a matter of the heart, not of externals. Remember, that unimpressive mission agency representative you meet is a person of distinction in the eyes of God.

But for many of us, the problem lies in the opposite direction. You may feel so overwhelmed by the accomplishments of those you meet that you're asking, "Who would want me?"

A commonplace fisherman once asked a similar question. He and his friends had slaved away for a whole night and hadn't caught a single fish. The next morning who but a land-loving carpenter should lead them out into deep water and instruct them in their own art. Come on now.

But the next thing they knew, their two boats were bulging with fish. Amazement seized this ordinary fisherman. Overwhelmed by his inadequacy and lack of faith, he cried, "Go away from me, Lord; I am a sinful man!"

The Lord's reply? "Don't be afraid; from now on you will catch men" (Luke 5:1-11). Who would want you? The Lord of the harvest, that's who.

And He isn't the only one. Hundreds of mission agencies are on the lookout for ordinary fishermen. By plunging in and beginning constructive dialogue, you can find a way to serve.

Jargon

Mission agency: a Christian organization helping to further God's work in the world. *Mission board* and *sending agency* are virtually the same thing. *Para-church* refers to a Christian organization independent of any church denominational structures.

Term: can refer to the length of a missionary's time commitment to a mission organization. Many career missionaries serve successive terms of two to five years. Often they spend a period of months in their home countries between terms, usually called a *furlough.* A *short term* can be as short as two weeks or as long as three years.

Deputation: commonly refers to the prayer and financial support rallying that career and short-term missionaries do before leaving for the field and during furloughs.

The field: short for *the mission field.* A field is anywhere that missionaries do their work. Regrettably, *field* sounds like it's out in the country or on a farm. Most mission situations are not farms, and are usually urbanized to some extent. A *field director* is one who oversees those who are working together in a particular country, people group, or location.

Support: the finances and prayer you will need to ask others to give for your trip. A *supporter* is one who gives and prays. A *support team* is the group of people who supports you. They may or may not know each other.

Unreached peoples: essentially "unchurched" peoples lacking an indigenous, evangelizing church-planting movement. Without such a movement, the people within these groups will likely never hear and obey the Gospel. People within these groups can be defined by ethno-linguistic factors or by socioeconomic realities.

National: any person who is from the country to which you are going. The nationals on your short term are those who call the country you visit their home. The *national leaders* are local people who are leading the church or mission. A *national church* is one that is led by national leaders.

International: what we call a national when he comes to our country.

Expatriate: someone who has left his or her home country to live and work in another country. When we visit another country, we call ourselves *expatriates* or *expats* for short.

Candidate: someone who has applied to a mission agency. The *candidate secretary* is the one who corresponds with people who apply to a mission. Some agencies gather candidates interested in career service at a week or two of *candidate school* to orient them to the agency and to evaluate each candidate for acceptance. Once accepted by the mission board, the candidate is called an *appointee*.

Missions committee: a specific group of people that oversees the missionary activity of the church. Theyoften has responsibility to allocate money for missions as well as to educate the entire church to support missionaries. Some churches have a *missions pastor* .

Relief: the urgent provision of resources to reduce suffering resulting from a natural or man-made disaster.

Development: a process enabling a community to provide for its own needs, beyond former levels, with dignity and justice.

Indigenous: native; originating in and having characteristics of a certain place or country. *Indigenous music* is usually created by nationals in their local style.

Church planting: means starting new churches.

Tentmaker: a cross-cultural witness who works at a paying, usually secular, job overseas. Often they are able to gain entry into *"closed" countries* which restrict traditional mission efforts. Tentmakers rarely make tents for a living, like the apostle Paul did, but they all should have the intention to further God's work.

Third World: Years ago, the United States and "free" Europe came to be called the West. Eastern bloc countries, such as the Soviet Union and other communist nations, formed a Second World. A good chunk of the lands formerly colonized by European powers came to be dubbed as the Third World. Third-World countries are typically underdeveloped economically by western standards. Recently, someone from the Third World, not realizing the history of the term, said, "Wait a minute, we're not even second. We want to be called the *Two-thirds World*, since two-thirds of the world's population lies in these countries." The Third World is now sometimes referred to as the Two-thirds World.

Itinerant: refers to people or ministries that travel from place to place.

Incarnational: living as much like and with the people to whom you're ministering as you are able. Just as Christ took on our flesh (*incarnate* means "to en-flesh") and culture to serve us, so cross-cultural missionaries often aspire to enter the culture and struggles of the people they desire to serve.

Contextualize: putting the truths of God into the context of the local culture. This involves seeing how one's own culture colors understanding of biblical truths, and then taking the unvarnished truth and applying it in another culture.

8

Bridge Building

Link your short term with your local church

by Paul Borthwick

Paul Borthwick, Minister of Missions at Grace Chapel in Lexington, Massachusetts, has sent over 400 youth and adults out on 60 short-term teams since 1978. He has also written eight books, including **A Mind For Missions,** **Youth and Missions,** *and* **How to Be a World-Class Christian.**

Diane's short-term missions experience left her feeling a little flat. It had all seemed great at the outset—a good mission agency, excellent financial support from her family and a few friends, and a fair amount of enthusiasm from her college peers. But when she arrived on the field, she sensed just how alone she was. Her family wrote regularly, but others seemed to forget about her, or so she felt. When she returned home, no one seemed interested in the intense experiences she'd had in a new culture. Her aloneness made her think, *I don't know if I'll ever go into missions again.*

Bob and Louise had a very different experience. Rather than going with an independent program, they decided to go through their church-affiliated short-term program. Their feelings of frustration came at the start of the summer: *Why do we have to do all of this paperwork? Why do we have to meet with the missions committee? When we're so ready to go, why does it seem that our church is dragging its feet?*

They spent time developing relationships with people in their church. After a special send-off service, Bob and Louise were taken to the airport by a dozen friends from the church.

During the summer, letters came regularly. They never felt the same sort of aloneness Diane felt because there were constant reminders that they weren't alone; their church was behind them. They returned two months later to an airport reception crowded with church members toting "Welcome Home" signs. Several expressed anticipation about hearing their reports. At the close of their experience, Bob and Louise thought, *Wow! Let's do this again.*

Although Diane and Bob and Louise are extreme (though true) cases, the basic reason for their contrasting summers was their relationship with a sending church.

Why Should I Work With My Church?

Let's be realistic; sometimes the local church doesn't seem too desirable. In some ways, it's easier just to go than to stay around and try to build relationships with people who may not seem supportive of missions.

There are at least three good reasons to spend the time needed to build bridges to the local church.

First, it's *biblical.* Jesus promises that the Church will prevail against the gates of hell (Matt. 16:18). The book of Acts shows the Church in action to fulfill the Great Commission through establishing churches. Missionaries are sent to establish churches, not to make solitary converts. If we ignore the local church in our own culture, what will we have to offer the local church in another?

Second, it's *practical.* Whether or not we want to admit it, our local church has plenty to offer in the sending process. Financial and prayer support are the most basic means of involvement, but people we know are crucial, too. They can best advise us on what we need to learn for a short-term assignment.

Finally, a short-term missionary can be a tremendous missions *catalyst* to the sending church. Most of us would admit that the local church (in general) is not fulfilling a strategic missions function. The solution, however, is not to circumvent the church in order to get to the field; the solution is to get involved enough so that we can build our missions vision into others.

Ways to Work With Your Church

Churches are different and churches change. Know your church. Many short-termers miss out on great opportunities to base their effort in their home church simply because they don't explore all the opportunities. Here are three ways to work with your church:

Local church-based programs. Some churches now develop their own programs for short-term missions. Instead of going through an independent group, consider the church program. In so doing, you establish a partnership with your sending body.

Denominational programs. You may be surprised to discover some of the programs directed by your denomination. In most cases, your local church will relax and more eagerly support you as you link with these kinds of short terms. There are a few situations in which denominational programs are known to be weak. Your local church leaders are key in helping to introduce you to your denomination.

Official church backing. The best option for you may be a stint with an independent agency, but with solid church backing through a missions committee or similar structure which can officially send you. Some short-termers are also launching out as tentmakers with no connection with an independent agency. It's all the more crucial that short-term tentmakers seek substantial support and encouragement, even though they may not need finances. There are usually ways to gain the counsel and backing of leaders in your church.

Build Bridges to Your Church

How can we rise to the challenge of involving our church in short-term missions? Consider these seven bridge builders.

Bridge-builder One: Communicate. Involve people in your church from the outset. Get them praying as the site and agency are selected. Ask for advice (and listen to it). If we're communicating with our church and pastor months before we go out, everyone will have a greater sense of being involved in our sending (and, correspondingly, in our financial and prayer support).

Bridge-builder Two: Learn the church's channels. One recent source observed that 48 percent of career missionaries sent in the last five years had short-term experience prior to their career commitment. Interpretation? Short-term experience may be one step toward full-term mission service.

With this in mind, it's critically important to learn how the sending church works, not just for short-term, but for long-term relationships. Becoming familiar with the faithful prayer partners, discovering the ways to apply for financial support, and getting to know the church leadership are all part of the bridge-building process. Knowing how the church operates can save frustration in future communications.

Bridge-builder Three: Submit. After reading Acts 13:1-3 and Michael Griffith's book, *Who Really Sends the Missionary?* (Moody Press, 1974), I became convinced that I should work through our elders and submit a decision to them regarding a short-term assignment in Hong Kong. When I asked for their blessing, I assumed that they would give it. To my surprise, they unanimously decided I shouldn't go. (They knew I needed to finish school first.) I was crushed, angry, and amazed, and for the first time, I had to learn what it was to live under authority.

Perhaps submission is the hardest of the bridge-builders, but whether it's easy or hard isn't the issue. The issue is whether we want to be sent out under the authority that God has ordained, even when that authority disagrees with what we think. There are, regretfully, those rare times when church leaders aren't faithful to scriptural priorities. Would-be missionaries have sometimes been restrained by church leaders who hold convictions unfavorable to biblical mission. If this is your situation, seek out several senior advisers and follow their counsel.

Bridge-builder Four: Recruit people to pray. You can't sit back in the hope that people will come to you; you need to go after them. Ask the pastor to include you in the pastoral prayer. Get interviewed. Recruit people to pray.

Bridge-builder Five: Involve people financially. One of the attractions of a short-term experience is the low cost. You might be able to pay for it from your savings, or perhaps relatives will foot the bill. This may be the fastest way to get support, but it isn't the best way. Prayer support, letters, and a sense of teamwork all benefit when many people are involved financially. Why not involve many people with small gifts?

Bridge-builder Six: Ask the church for a commissioning. The prayer witness of the Holy Spirit in Acts 13 helped give Paul and Barnabas the spiritual energy they needed to go out as missionaries. You need the same. In an all-congregation church service, you should get commissioned for your short-term assignment by the church leadership. Prayer—and in some cases the laying on of hands—will provide a strong sense of spiritual identification between you and your sending church.

Bridge-builder Seven: Report back. I remember a short-termer who didn't stay in touch with me during his first two years of college—until he needed money to serve for a summer in India as a short-term missionary. The church where I'm a pastor supported him, wrote to him while he was there, and prayed for him. Now he's back at school, but I still haven't heard from him. Such lack of response discourages our church from sponsoring short-term involvement.

Don't wait until you get back to stay in touch. It may take careful planning, but correspondence and communication with your church will bond you with your senders. People want to know how their prayers are being answered, and it's your responsibility to tell them. They need specifics for their intercession, and you can relay these needs by letter, postcard, telegram, or phone call.

You have a great privilege and responsibility to build bridges into your church which will help you better understand God's strategy for missions and help your church fulfill its God-given purpose as a world-changing sender.

9

Get Blessed Before Blasting Off

How to talk to your pastor before you go

by Chris Stanton

*Chris Stanton is the author of **The Mission Bridge Manual**, a "how to" book on establishing a training school for missions in the local church. He is on staff with Youth With A Mission in Los Angeles.*

Many people leave for short-term missions in an under-blessed state. They may have good motives for going, decent preparation, enough cash, and fine spiritual maturity with all the right gifts. But often, their venture comes off a little flat because they weren't "blessed" enough.

By getting blessed, I don't mean getting a warm, spiritual, glowing feeling. The kind of blessing short-termers need is the spiritual backing of their church leaders. Too often, pastors are approached for financial support a few days before departure, without even knowing where the short-termer is going, who they are going with, what they are going to do, or why. Sometimes the pastor is hit up for finances without even knowing who's asking.

You need the blessing of your pastor and other spiritual leaders before you go, because you need the spiritual power boost that comes with the total backing of your fellowship leaders. No matter how simple the short term looks to you, you can't do it alone. You can actually tap into the spiritual energy of your entire church by getting the blessing of your pastor.

Getting blessed is more than getting financial backing. It means that the pastor and the church are identifying themselves with you. That's why some church leaders place their hands on and pray for missionaries as they send them out. That's just one style of expressing the reality of blessing. The important thing is to get significant spiritual support, regardless of how it's expressed. Don't think of the blessing as some super-spiritual magic event. It just means that your pastor and other leaders are wholeheartedly behind you.

The following isn't going to sound like good advice at first:

Don't tell your pastor that you're going on a short-term mission. That's right, don't *tell* him. Instead, *ask* him. Ask your pastor about your short-term ideas. Your pastor should hear of the *possibility* of your going before he hears of the *fact* that you are going. He should be involved in praying, thinking, planning through, and even "supporting through" your decision.

It's up to you to begin. Don't wait for your pastor to grab you in the pew and say, "Isn't it time you went to Nigeria?" You have to share your dreams with your pastor. Make an appointment to visit with him, and be ready to communicate as many details as you know about the expedition. Go to him and ask for his prayers and spiritual support. Listen to his questions, concerns, and fears about your mission adventure.

Here you'll encounter a paradox: you have to be as clear as you can about your short-term aspirations and plans, but at the same time, you need to stay flexible to postpone or change your plans.

Your pastor can't bless an endeavor he doesn't know about or fully understand. Give him plenty of time (days or weeks). Your pastor can be a wealth of understanding, wisdom, and knowledge. Listen to his counsel, think through his questions carefully, and follow through on any suggestions he might have. Be prepared to make a clear presentation of how you're expecting your trip to be financed. This will give your pastor the opportunity to make suggestions as to whether or not the church would be in a position to help you. Don't be afraid of pressuring the pastor to give support. You can feel free to ask, as long as you leave him the freedom to respond. Respect his grasp of the big financial picture of the church.

Go, and go with the blessing. Pray for it. Ask for it. Even if the church can't help you financially, it's important that you ask your pastor for whatever blessing he can give. It will add to your mission and to your personal and spiritual life. Be grateful for it, and return the blessing to those who have blessed you. Return with a good report of the extension of the Kingdom of God.

10
Honoring Parents

How to obey your parents
and the Great Commission at the same time

by David M. Howard

Dr. David M. Howard, International Director of World Evangelical Fellowship in Singapore, served 15 years in Colombia and Costa Rica with Latin American Mission. He also served as Director of Urbana '73 and Urbana '76.

He was my best friend in college. Living together in the dorm, we often spent time in prayer and Bible study together. He was a missionary candidate who had godly parents and whose vision was burning and contagious.

One day as we were about to pray, he said, "Dave, I have no doubt that God wants me overseas. But my parents think I would be wasting my talents to go to some remote tribe when I could be more effectively used among youth here at home." He went on to tell me how he loved and respected his parents and didn't want to displease or dishonor them. He wondered how he could honor them and still be obedient to God's call.

This was a major dilemma. We prayed together about it, and one day he sat down and wrote these lines to his parents:

"Grieve not, then, if your sons seem to desert you; but rejoice, rather, seeing the will of God done gladly. Remember how the Psalmist described children? He said that they were as a heritage from the Lord, and that every man should be happy who had his quiver full of them (Ps. 127:3-5). And what is a quiver full of but arrows? And what are arrows for but to shoot? So, with the strong arm of prayer, draw the bowstring back and let the arrows fly—all of them, straight at the enemy's host."

His parents got the point. They placed their son in the bow of prayer, pulled back the bowstring, and prayed him out to a remote Indian tribe in Ecuador. He never came back. He was murdered by the Indians he'd gone to reach, but the testimony of his life and witness goes on to this day. His name was Jim Elliot.

Not all of you have parents who will agree to pray you out in obedience to God's call. Some of you, like Jim, have Christian parents who don't understand why you're considering overseas service, even on a short-term basis. Others have parents, Christian or non-Christian, who will oppose such an idea. How do you handle this? May I venture a few practical suggestions?

Pray With Your Parents

As Jim prayed about how to reconcile obedience to God with honor to his parents, the Lord led him to a Scripture to answer the dilemma both for him and for them. God may not choose to answer your prayer in the same way, but the first and most basic step in any problem is to spread it out before the Lord.

If your parents are Christians, why not ask them to pray with you about this decision? In this way, they become involved in the decision-making process and will be more likely to understand and support you.

Honor Your Parents

Paul reminds us that the fifth commandment—"Honor your father and mother"—is also "the first commandment with a promise" (Eph. 6:2). The promise is "...so that you may live long in the land the Lord your God is giving you" (Ex. 20:12).

No other aspect of your relationship with your parents is more important than honoring them. It's so important that God includes it in the very limited list of ten simple commandments that form the basis of our relationship to God and to the world.

The rest of this article will be nothing more than an elaboration on how to honor your parents, especially as you venture you into a new "land" that the Lord may be "giving you."

Show Love to Your Parents

Whether or not your parents are Christians is irrelevant to whether or not you honor them. And there's no greater way to honor your parents than to show them that you love them. Parents need love just as much (and sometimes more) than children do. Children are often unaware of how much their parents crave their love. They may feel that their parents "have it all together" and that they have no deep emotional needs, especially those relating to their children. Nothing could be further from the truth.

Children play a very key role in this area. I remember when our youngest son, with whom I'd had some difficulty in relating during his teenage years, said after his first year in college, "Dad, I don't think I've ever told you this before, but I think you're a great dad, and I love you." Surprise and gratitude overwhelmed me. Don't be hesitant to tell your parents—verbally and in actions—that you love them. You say they already know this? They may be plagued with doubts, so tell them this all-important truth.

Spend Time With Your Parents

Demonstrate your love to your parents by spending time with them. Parents want time with their children. My elderly mother lived with us during part of her final years. Her body was weak and her mind was confused, but she knew me clearly. One afternoon, I went into her room to talk with her. She seemed unsettled. I said, "Mother, is there anything I can do for you, or is there something you want?" She replied, "I want you." I realized that in the loneliness of her confined and confused life, she wanted the presence of her son more than anything else.

Although your parents may not be at that stage yet, there's probably nothing they want or enjoy more than having their children with them. Demonstrating your love by spending quality time with them is one of the greatest things you can do to prepare for the inevitable separation when you go overseas.

Involve Your Parents

As you prepare for an overseas assignment, whether short- or long-term, you need to learn all you can about the country to which you're going. Why not involve your parents in learning, too? Help them feel the excitement and anticipation of what it will mean to live and work in a new culture. Help them understand what a broadening and educational experience this will be.

Perhaps you can persuade them to read one or more of the books you should be reading in preparation for your overseas service. This will help them to understand better what you're thinking and what you will be facing. It may also help alleviate some of the fears or questions they will have. Fear is often based on ignorance, and anything that will clear up ignorance will help remove fears.

Perhaps someone from that country—missionary or national—could visit your parents to help them understand what your life will be like. Personal contact, especially if it's with someone with whom you might be working, will alleviate fears and strengthen your parents' understanding.

Keep in Touch With Your Parents

When you go overseas, be careful to keep in touch with your

parents. I know how easy it is to become so bogged down in the pressures of work that you feel you have no time for correspondence. But few things are more important than maintaining that lifeline with your parents. Most areas of the world today have good, direct-dial telephone communications. The investment of an occasional phone call will pay rich dividends in strengthening the all-important relationship with your parents.

Why not invite them to visit you on location? Nothing can take the place of a visit in helping your parents to understand and appreciate life in another culture.

Demonstrate Your Commitment to the Call of God

Finally, be certain that your commitment to God and to His claims on your life isn't hidden. Even if your parents are non-Christians, you shouldn't hide the fact that Jesus Christ takes first place in your life. Your desire to go overseas is primarily a response to His last commission to take the Gospel to every people and nation.

Your parents may not fully understand—much less sympathize with—this desire of yours. But they can't help but respect your commitment to the Person who means more to you than anyone or anything else. Even if they oppose your going, they must see that this is based on your obedience to the commands of the One who is now Lord of your life.

Remember the Lord said: "No one who has left home or wife or brothers or parents or children for the sake of the Kingdom of God will fail to receive many times as much in this age, and in the age to come, eternal life" (Luke 18:29-30).

11

God's Pattern of Provision

Understanding the biblical precedent
for support raising

by Roger Randall

Roger Randall, director of International University Resources for Campus Crusade for Christ and co-founder of the Worldwide Student Network, works extensively with short-term missions around the world.

So, you're going to have to raise support? Maybe you've quaked at the very thought or really wondered if you can do it. Well, you're not the first one to wonder that.

Many have gone into the support-raising adventure with fear and trembling, and most have found great success in support raising. You can, too. A good way to start is by understanding the biblical rationale behind the practice. Once you understand that, you'll be better able to raise support with boldness and confidence.

The First Financial Plan

Nearly 3,300 years ago, God designed a financial plan that would provide salaries and benefits to His workers. In the book of Numbers, God called the Levites to be His first "professional" ministers, instructing them to rely on Him for their financial stability. There were plenty of qualified, motivated laymen (such as Moses, Joshua, and Caleb) to work on the tabernacle, but God was looking for more than part-time help. He wanted to meet the demanding spiritual needs of the nation, needs that couldn't be met by even the most dedicated workers in their spare time alone.

While the nation of Israel worked the land and faced the financial uncertainties brought on by drought, disease, and famine, the Lord promised to provide for the Levites through the tithes and offerings of their countrymen. The people of God were to support the full-time ministers of God.

A Covenant of Interdependence

After Christ came, God established a new covenant whereby any believer (not just those in the family of Levi) could serve Him in full-time ministry. Jesus, who was a carpenter, could have funded His ministry by building furniture or repairing carts and tables. But as far as we know, He didn't. As Jesus went out ministering, He relied on people such as Mary, Martha, and Lazarus who helped "...support him out of their own means" (Luke 8:3). Jesus had financial supporters.

When Christ commissioned His followers, He gave them the spiritual authority to minister and told them to trust Him for their physical provisions (Matt. 10:9,10). Jesus gave specific directions to His disciples which forced them to depend on others for their needs. They were to accept gifts from others, as Jesus said, "...eating and drinking whatever they give you; for the worker deserves his wages..." (Luke 10:4-7). A laborer in God's Kingdom is truly worthy of being paid for his service. The Early Church workers lived on a system of support similar to that which God established for the Levites.

The apostle Paul writes in I Corinthians 9:14, "In the same way, the Lord has commanded that those who preach the gospel should receive their living from the gospel." He explains that God set up a system of financial support for His workers. He also writes that even though he had the right to be supported by the Corinthians, he chose to make tents. This was an exception, however, to Paul's usual method of ministry.

Paul wanted to make sure the Corinthians to whom he preached had no reason to question his motives. He chose to live on a smaller salary and take less from the Corinthians in order to validate his character, his faith, and his ministry. With the Corinthian church, Paul may have supplemented his income by sewing canvas, but he did rely on gifts from supporters. Paul willingly received financial support from other Christians and churches, and he asked for support. In Romans, he wrote, "When I go to Spain...I hope...to have you assist me on my journey" (Rom. 15:24). The original Greek in this verse confirms that Paul was requesting money.

John also referred to God's people supporting their own. "It was for the sake of the Name that they went out, receiving no help from the pagans. We ought therefore to show hospitality to such men so that we may work together for the truth" (III John 7,8).

Living by Faith Today

Raising support doesn't make you holier than others. There's nothing you can do or fail to do that will make you more spiritual or alter your eternal position in Christ (Eph. 1:3-14, Rom. 6:5-9).

Many outstanding denominations and mission groups offer salaries to their missionaries, and the Lord is honoring their ministries. All Christians need to live by faith (II Cor. 5:7; Heb. 11:6) regardless of how they receive their paychecks.

The bottom line is that you need to be willing to do whatever the Lord asks you to do, or you won't be qualified for any missionary career (salaried or supported).

Most people find themselves a little uneasy as they approach the challenge of support raising. It seems to go against our American culture to depend on others—especially for finances. As Christians, we need to heed the strong scriptural warnings about conforming to our culture's values. We must remember that the Bible strongly states that accepting support gifts is part of God's economy.

In this sense, raising support is a matter of obedience to God's work and calling, not of following your feelings. If God calls you to a supported ministry position, then He will provide everything you need to fulfill your ministry, including emotional strength and perseverance (Phil. 4:19; I Thess. 5:24).

For further study and consideration, see Numbers 1:45-54; Numbers 18; Deuteronomy 18:1-6; Jeremiah 29:11; Matthew 16:25; Luke 6:38; Luke 8:1-3; I Corinthians 9; John 15:16.

12

Have Fun Getting Funded

How to face the pitfalls and practices
of raising support

by Chris Stanton

Chris Stanton is the author of **The Mission Bridge Manual,** *a "How To" book on establishing a training school for missions in the local church. He is on staff with Youth With A Mission in Los Angeles.*

"This church is not going to pay for those kids to have a vacation in Europe," declared the flush-faced deacon, "even if they do call it a mission!"

If the hopes and dreams of a young generation of short-term missionaries hinged on the mindset of this deacon, not too many would be going on short-term missions this summer. We're grateful that most churches (and deacons) no longer maintain an attitude that missions is only for those with four to eight years of training. Today, many churches are willing to help support short-term missionaries if they can show that their mission will have an impact for the Kingdom of God.

Potential Pitfalls

Since most missionaries are financially supported by individuals and churches, one doesn't get too far along on his or her "mission planning" before the question of how to raise money arises. Let's look at some pitfalls of poor thinking when it comes to financing a short-term trip and then at some practical ways to get the job done.

Pitfall One: The Beggar Bugaboo

Somehow, support raising can seem like a sure way to turn off all your friends, offend your family, and ruin your reputation. Sometimes, important family members can howl about "my son, the religious beggar."

Don't believe the bad press. Support raising is not rattling a tin cup for spiritual welfare. It's team ministry. You're asking others to add their financial and prayer strength to the total effort of your mission group. If you do it well, you honor your friends and family by placing yourself in a dependent mode on them. In most people's experience, few friendships are paralyzed by a request for funds. Most friends draw closer. Many of us enjoy the privacy and independence of financing our own affairs. This can lead directly into the second pitfall, in which would-be missionaries put plans on hold to get a job to earn money for the total cost of their trip.

Pitfall Two: Checkbook Guidance

This term describes the method of determining your availability to be used by God on a short-term mission by looking at the bottom line of your checkbook, where it reads "Present Balance." The reasoning is that if you have the money, you'll go; if not, you won't. If every mission enterprise were determined by the present amount of available funds, not much would ever be accomplished in missions. (Just ask a seasoned missionary.)

Instead, give God the opportunity to go beyond your means. That's when this whole process gets exciting. That's when you know you're not just forcing your way onto the field but allowing God to provide for you and send you out.

Pitfall Three: Rich Uncle Syndrome

This syndrome strikes when a person thinks that one individual or organization will underwrite his or her mission. Although this may be possible for a select few, it can be a dangerous approach to God's work. Even if your past history tells you that your parents or someone else will cover your expenses, any short-term missionary who wishes to execute a mission with integrity needs to go to God for His strategy.

That strategy may demand that you go beyond the lone individual for your support. More people on your support team means more people influenced, involved in, and affected by your mission. If you want a delightful support-raising experience, build a loyal team of friends to pray, work for, and rally around you during your support-raising process. They can help you brainstorm, mail prayer letters, do fund-raising projects—and they can provide a shoulder to cry on when the going gets rough.

Pitfall Four: Ignoring the Supernatural

As a training director of short-term missions for the past eight years, I've seen some wonderful and unusual ways God has provided money. As one mission leader says, "Where God leads, He feeds. Where He guides, He provides." The emphasis here is on

"He." Never give up, no matter how impossible the situation seems financially. Trust God. If He has prompted you to go, He will provide for you, as well.

Get it fresh in your mind that God is the Provider. He has the resources. Your responsibility is not to get money from people, but to get wisdom and strength from God and depend on Him.

Positive Steps

Let's look at some positive steps of action to prepare yourself to receive the needed finances for your mission. Be sure that you never look at this wonderful opportunity to raise support and involve yourself with others as something negative or as a burden. Try to put your finger on your misgivings and questions. Talk it over with someone you trust who has done it before.

1. Pray. Pray that money in. Long before actually counting the money that comes in, you should have counted on it, by faith. Prayer is the only way to keep from fret and worry.

Some pray until they have God's assurance—a deep conviction that He will provide. This may take some time, but it's well worth the work. Once you are sure that God's desire is to provide for you as His child, you can raise support with confidence.

2. Make a budget. Know exactly how much the mission will cost. Most agencies already have set budgets for their short-termers. If not, develop your own. Don't forget to list food, transportation, toiletries, unexpected emergencies, and gifts. (You should consider bringing a small gift back to those who helped you get there.)

Type out your budget so you can be prepared to share it with those who may ask how much your short term will cost. Your budget will speak to them of your seriousness about this trip.

3. Develop a financial strategy. List all the resources available to people who might support you. This will help you consider how to spur people on to give creatively and sacrificially. Do this sensitively, of course. You may have more resources than you realize. Consider breaking your piggy bank of personal savings. Why not sell some stuff (stereo, car, other non-essentials)? You might be able to work an extra job.

Ask God for a clear support-raising strategy. Your agency or church may have guidelines you must follow as you raise support. As a representative of their ministry, it's important that you follow them. There is almost always some flexibility built into such systems, so don't overlook the consultation of your pastor and other mission leaders to help you think through the special needs of your support-raising strategy. Brainstorm and write down all the ways you can think of to raise the money.

Write down the names of those you might ask to become involved financially in your ministry. This list will help you make sure you don't miss any potential givers. Be very open minded while you do this. You'd be surprised how many people have old neighbors and great-aunts as their most loyal supporters. Be sure to contact parents, friends, relatives, business associates, your church, clubs you belong to, or even past employers.

4. Be prepared to make a presentation. One of the best ways to let people know about your short term is through face-to-face conversation or public presentation. If God directs you to share your financial needs with others, be prepared to make an excellent presentation. Here are a few essentials to cover:

- Who you are.
- Where you're going.
- Why you're going.
- Who you're going with (organization).
- What you expect from the mission.
- What you expect to give to others through the mission.
- How long it will take.
- How much it will cost.
- How much money is still needed.
- Your need for people to pray about providing financial support.

Some people have convictions about not sharing specifics on their financial need. That's okay. Certainly act out of your convictions or the policy of your mission agency. I think it's wise to be very clear to potential supporters what your needs are and just how much they might give. In my experience, it really frustrates supporters to not know how much they're expected to give or if you really need the support. It rarely ever puts them off to be asked directly. You won't lose friends. People can relax around you, knowing just how much you need and knowing that you know just how much they can do to help.

When you give a presentation, be sure to intersperse a lot of stories and anecdotes about yourself and your task. Don't talk too much. And always leave time for people to respond.

Tips for an Effective Support-Raising Presentation

- Don't rely on letters. Letters alone are the least effective means of communicating your mission and your need. Statistics show a two percent response. If you must send a letter, make sure it's followed by a phone call and a specific request for a prayerful response.
- Make a personal visit. This is most effective, with a sixty percent favorable response. Call first. Look sharp. Show up on time, and keep it short and to the point.
- Telephone calls are second only to personal presentations, with a forty percent effectiveness rate. The same principles that apply to a face-to-face presentation apply over the phone. Once you've told them what you want, be sure to send follow-up information.
- One good method is to use a response card. Your donors will need to know pertinent information like how to give, where to send the check, how to get in contact with you, and whether tax credit can be received. Give them a prayer reminder such as a picture of yourself with dates, times, places, and the type of ministry in which you'll be involved.

We've barely scratched the surface of the whole ministry of support raising, but this should provide a few suggestions of how to begin. Be ready for a challenge; be ready for a blessing.

Go!

You might remember it as the best and the worst time of your life. Go with confidence that God is giving you all you need to face the challenges ahead.

13

Maximum Short-Term Mission

Making the most of your short term

by Steven C. Hawthorne

Steven C. Hawthorne has led short-term teams in Asia and the Middle East. He presently serves with Antioch Network, an organization serving churches sending teams to unreached peoples.

My great-aunt went to Africa as a missionary on a steamboat. Everybody in her generation who went overseas did it by boat. I guess that's the classic way to go. It almost seems like the biblical way to move out for mission work. Paul certainly did a lot of moving by boat. Even Jesus used boats to get around. One thing about missions in the steamboat era: people went for a lifetime or not at all.

But today, for the most part, we fly to mission assignments. Almost any place on earth can be reached within a day by airplane. And air travel has opened up a new thing in missions: the short term. Now people can head overseas for two years, two months, or two weeks.

There were early skeptics. You can understand why some mission leaders worried about fielding a horde of "sunshine soldiers" who get in the way for the summer, then go AWOL for life from missions. Their fears have been allayed a great deal by the outstanding performance of most short-termers. Most of the people leaving the home shores for a lifetime have been overseas before. Even the most staid and traditional missions organizations have realized that short terms are a great way to recruit new workers.

But short-term workers are still a new and sometimes underused resource in missions. We have yet to fathom all that short terms can mean in fulfilling the Great Commission.

Why am I telling you all this? You're probably not a mission executive. You're probably someone who has considered going overseas, at least for a short time and perhaps for a lifetime. (Perhaps you're like me; you have already been out of the country on a short term and may be wondering what comes next.)

I encourage you to take responsibility to make the most of your short term. Here are five actions that almost anyone on any short term can take to maximize the entire expedition.

Experience

Experience the culture of another people. Guess who's shocking you with their culture? The people. Culture shock is really people shock. Don't hunker down and hide out in foxholes of American hotels to take cover from all the barrages of weird food, blaring traffic, and pestiferous kids. Get out of the trenches and love some people. If you withdraw from the people of the host culture, you might as well go home.

Plan to get to know some of the people as well as you can. You'll be frustrated with the language barrier. (Welcome to missions.) But don't let it stop you from using whatever silly gimmick you can to befriend someone in that culture. It simply isn't possible to experience the culture without relationships. It may cost you some pride and time, but don't fool yourself into thinking that you know what it's like overseas just because you have physically been there. That's just plain old tourism.

Don't hide out in the confines of the church, where Christians constitute a little subculture. Befriend a non-Christian. You might discover why there are so many of them.

In the same way, get acquainted with a diversity of peoples and brackets of society. Fearlessly immerse yourself in need. Poverty isn't contagious. Your hosts might urge you to stay away from certain neighborhoods and people, but take them with you unless there is some genuine reason to fear for your safety. Usually there isn't. Better yet, don't just make forays out into the poor communities. Make them the focus of your relationships. The poor can usually tell you almost anything you need to know about the more well-to-do, but it doesn't work the other way around. Rich folks are usually embarrassingly ignorant of the impoverished.

Let me warn you about going relational. You probably won't be overseas long enough to experience classic culture shock, but it's dangerous to truly begin to experience another culture. It sort of ruins you for the joy of profligate waste and the fun of unchecked individualism we enjoy so much here at home.

It can bother you to see how easily you forget the weekly TV schedule. Having the right kind of shoes or the correct width necktie becomes less important. And just for a moment, you can defy the gravity of your own culture and find yourself not caring if you ever top a salary of $100,000 per year, or if you break 100,000 on Ms. Pac Man. What begins to matter most is God's glory in a world of people.

Cross-cultural experience helps you prize people over things, value friendships over your own frustrations, and put your plans into God's hands. So I warn you, watch out for true experience of other cultures. It will irrevocably change you.

Explore

Explore the work of the missionary. Most short terms are designed to expose you to what it is like to be a missionary. That suits many short-termers, because that's why they've come. It's hard to imagine yourself as a missionary if you've never seen one in action.

Good luck watching missionaries. They're notoriously hard to view in action on the field. Instead of getting exposed to the *work* of a missionary, many short-termers get exposed to the *life* of the missionary. Out of concern for you, the missionary may emphasize daily stuff like how to ride the bus, or emergency things like how to get to the doctor.

So it's up to you to find out what these people really do. Inquire about their goals and how they know if they've reached them. Probe into their story, looking for the key factors of their success. Explore how the non-Christian world perceives the missionary.

Be ready for some surprises and disappointments. It turns out that most missionaries retain their humanity and find themselves capable of the most dismal, blind failure, and at the same time, demonstrate excellence beyond your furthest Mother Teresa expectations. Don't embarrass your host missionaries too greatly by discovering that they don't accomplish too much. Instead, focus on strengths.

Make sure you understand why the missionary does what he or she does. Don't be judgmental. You don't have to evaluate. Simply aim at getting a vision of what the missionary is trying to do. Above all, pray with the missionaries to feel what is on their hearts.

Extend

Extend the work of the Gospel. Almost any short term will encourage you to experience culture and explore the missionary career. But few missions will go beyond these and deliberately encourage you to do significant evangelism during your admittedly brief stay.

Everyone knows that you will change more than the country

will, but develop some goals of furthering the Gospel while there. No covert operations, please. You could really blow the missionary's carefully established entry into the community.

Billy Graham you're not. Don't plan on changing an entire city or country during your stint overseas. Try praying that one or two people to make radical steps toward the Kingdom while you're there. There's a lot you can do without the local language if you team up with missionaries or nationals. A national worker told me once to go wild in befriending and evangelizing English speakers in an out-and-out unreached city. "You win their ears, and we will win their hearts," he said.

Your assignment may not be "front-line communicator." There are many ways to serve and push the whole Gospel movement forward. But don't be content to baby-sit or type or fix cars or paint buildings, even if the main purpose for your coming was to serve in those ways. Do your assigned job, but press for a way and some time to be involved in communicating God's love with someone who doesn't know Him.

Exchange

Exchange insights, strengths, and love with national Christians. Most short-termers eke out a modicum of bewildered respect for their national hosts. But few break through their own shyness, busyness, or just plain old prejudice to interact with some of the finest disciples alive. These national Christian leaders are often busy without showing it, so be careful with timing.

I've had senior saints patiently and eagerly listen to me deliver my favorite sermonettes. That's not what I mean by exchanging God's love. Don't talk so much. Listen. Express interest in hearing their story and the story of their family. Tell a few stories from your own experience, and pretty soon you'll be trading insights and truths that will truly stretch you.

Pray with your national co-workers. Exploit any chance to watch them minister to their own people. Sharing like this will widen your discipleship like few other relationships.

Prepare yourself as Paul did. Anticipating his visit with Christians in Rome, he was ready to give and receive, "...that I may impart to you some spiritual gift to make you strong—that is, that you and I may be mutually encouraged by each other's faith" (Rom. 1:11,12).

Once again, let me warn you. Relationships like this could spoil you for the fun of squabbling over the non-essentials of the Gospel back home. Meeting with Christians under trees in Asian refugee camps might mellow the discussion about new carpet in the youth wing. Modestly adorned, but altogether topless, deaconesses in New Guinea might make you more disinterested in discussing what is proper attire for church at home. Hearing a whole village in Africa recount how God cast out demons and raised the dead might soften your position on spiritual gifts. When acquainted with other expressions of the Gospel, you can begin to see more clearly what is wine and what is mere wineskin.

You need to carefully select your mission for its goals, activities, and flexibility to do the best experiencing, exploring, extending, and exchanging. Regardless of the team with which you work, it's up to you to make the most of it.

Expose

Expose others to what God is doing. It's commonly held that short terms are good for would-be missionaries so they can get *exposed* to a cross-cultural environment.

I think some short-term missionaries ought to be apprehended for indecent exposure. I'm not talking about the guys who make fools of themselves in Thailand by wearing shorts or the women who fail to wear saris in India. No, I'm talking about the lousy job some of us do in exposing our home churches to the needs and opportunities in the places we have been.

I'll grant you that most churches show only perfunctory and passing interest in being challenged to missions involvement. But that's precisely my point. How can churches ever become whole-heartedly motivated for the Great Commission unless they're challenged by their own people? Who can do it better than the short-termer?

If short-term experiences get locked in personal diaries, they are lost as challenges to the Church. Every short-termer should leave home prepared to not just report the travelogue and say a dutiful "thank you," but also to agitate on the grassroots level in the Church for greater commitment to missions.

Aim your most vigorous mobilization efforts at small groups and personal friends. When you get a chance to report to the entire congregation, resist the temptation to lambast them for their spiritual sloth. Emphasize the opportunities to take joint action that lie before the Church. This means you have to be something of a visionary. Go ahead. If you don't do the dreaming, who will?

Work for the long haul. Without being obnoxious, be persistent in little ways, such as injecting a prayer request for the country in group prayer meetings. Work toward sending someone else on a short term to the same place. Keep up correspondence with the folks overseas, and keep your church updated.

Maximize the potential of your short term. Stop treating it as if it were a private rite of passage. If you jump on a short term like a Disneyland ride and passively wait to get exposed and experienced, don't be surprised if you're disappointed. Mission commitment doesn't happen like getting a suntan. Don't go if you aren't ready for your life to change. And if you go, make it a world-changer.

14

Brokenness

Short accounts in short-term mission work

by George Verwer

George Verwer, founder and International Director of Operation Mobilisation, pioneered the work of O.M. on his first short term to Mexico in 1957.

Your level of humility and patience will be tested on a short-term mission. You're going to stand in lines, steaming mad, with smoke blowing out of your ears. There will be too much work and not enough people to do it. There won't be enough money. You'll encounter a complexity of problems and fiery darts from Satan that make things go wrong.

You'll experience strained relationships. Even Americans living on the same side of the Mason-Dixon line have miscommunication. Imagine what happens when we join hands North and South, throw in a few Canadians, add a few Mexicans, and go somewhere like Belgium where there are over 20 other nationalities.

What will it take to live in victory on a short-term mission? If we are going to make an impact on a hard, lost, doubting, skeptical, cynical world, it's going to mean being honest and open before God and others. It's going to take a stripping away of the window dressing. It's going to take brokenness.

Brokenness is not a word we use much, but we do find it in the Bible. In Psalm 51, written after Nathan confronted David about Bathsheba, David breaks before God: "Cleanse me with hyssop, and I will be clean; wash me, and I will be whiter than snow. Let me hear joy and gladness; let the bones you have crushed rejoice" (verses 7, 8). Later, he says, "The sacrifices of God are a broken spirit; a broken and contrite heart, O God, you will not despise" (verse 17).

We see a picture in the Old Testament of the potter molding a clay pot. When it doesn't come out the way he wants, he breaks it and starts again. For us, brokenness is humility's response to the touch of God. We break and say, "Lord, You're right; I'm wrong.

Your word is right; my idea is wrong."

I remember a phone call I made several years ago. I'd called John, a co-worker, about something that had gone wrong, and I'd given him a piece of my mind. (I really urge you to learn *not* to give away pieces of your mind; you can run out before you're 30.) Whatever I'd said on the phone had come across too strongly. As soon as I hung up the phone, the referee—the Holy Spirit—blew the whistle in my heart. I phoned John back, confronted the unkindness, and asked him for forgiveness.

We must listen to that referee. If we don't, God often lets us go on. He doesn't just rub out people because they refuse to deal with arrogance or subtle forms of pride in their lives. The mission field is full of uncrucified people. They've gone on, but they've brought leanness on themselves; they seldom bear much fruit.

As we draw closer to the Lord Jesus, and as we get more of the Scriptures burning in our hearts, we'll learn to keep short accounts before God. Often it happens without any fanfare; without even bowing our heads. We may be walking along the road and have an evil thought about a brother or sister. We don't have to roll in sackcloth and ashes. (Our cleaning bills could get very high.) We must simply repent instantly of what we've said in our hearts. The best way to be brought to repentance is to repent immediately, without anyone having to confront you.

You may find yourself arguing with God. That's okay, as long as you are bent and broken before the argument is over. I would challenge you, especially if you have a sharp tongue, to study the books of Proverbs and James about the control of the tongue. Believe God that your tongue may be crucified, and when it gets you into trouble, you'll hear the referee of the Holy Spirit, and you'll quickly apologize.

We must learn, as I John 1:7 teaches, to walk in the light with God and with each other. "But if we walk in the light, as he is in the light, we have fellowship with one another, and the blood of Jesus, his Son, purifies us from all sin." That's the only way we can have effective teamwork. There will be misunderstandings; we'll hurt and offend one another; but we'll still have fellowship if we walk in the light.

What does it mean to walk in the light with each other? It doesn't mean bondage to the letter of the Law. It doesn't mean setting yourself up as Mr. or Ms. Corrector, but it does mean dealing with the problems that arise.

We should first set an example of brokenness in our own lives. Brokenness is contagious. As one person breaks and acknowledges sin, other people get convicted. It's hard to pray with a broken person if you're stubborn and unrepentant.

Be willing to confess your own sin. You may think the other person is 90 percent wrong and you're only 10 percent wrong, but don't wait for them to apologize first. Go and confess. You may discover that the other person will be convicted. If not, don't respond in anger, "If you don't repent, I'm taking my repentance back." We're not playing a manipulative game.

Florence Allshorn said after years of missionary work, "If Christ cannot save me from those things that jar on my fellow missionaries, then I have but a thin message of salvation, and if I cannot help my English sister get through certain selfish attitudes which create unhappiness for myself or anyone else, how can I say that I have come to help my African or Indian sister get through hers?"

What does it mean to walk in the light with people from other cultures? Two principles have helped me immensely.

First, listen. Make that your motto, especially if you're a bigmouth like me. I can remember some very ugly scenes between American and British people, because we seem so alike, but we are so different.

As guests in other people's countries, we must be careful to use proper manners. We must ask lots of questions. It's very difficult to sit down at a meal without making a mistake, so I say, "Please, don't make a big thing of it, but if I'm doing something that's a little bit wrong, maybe you could correct me. I've just been in your country for a short time, and I'm trying to learn." Be quick to listen.

Second, be quick to say you're sorry. Be willing to confess your own sin. Don't wait for the other person to apologize first.

We often run into problems as Americans because in general, we're boisterous, we're loud, we think we're the best, and we go where angels would fear to tread. I've known short-termers who go into someone else's home, take a book off the shelf, and start reading it without asking. Some people are very sensitive to things like that.

I make many phone calls to apologize for my team. I say to the pastor who has hosted us, "If the team has done anything wrong, please forgive us. We're learning."

How vividly I remember one of our outreaches in Mexico. I had a fantastic desire to hand out literature, so we dumped tracts on churches. We manipulated pastors into taking 10,000 tracts when they didn't have a clue how they would give out 1,000. A year later, I went back to one of those churches where I'd delivered a lot of tracts. I saw those tracts and thought, *This is grieving the Spirit.* I went to that pastor and said, "Look, we gave you these tracts last summer, and look at this."

Here I was, a little American barely able to speak Spanish, telling off this pastor. He blew a fuse. (Don't presume the other guy is more broken than you.) I blew an American fuse, and he blew a Mexican fuse. He said some things to me—I think the word *gringo* came out (plus a couple of others)—but somehow, in the mercy of God, I realized I'd blown it. I humbled myself before that man, and I begged him to forgive me for the terrible things I'd said. We began to weep together, and another healthy relationship was born.

I believe that without a renewed emphasis on humility, brokenness, and repentance, much missionary work ends up hay and stubble. If you don't think your team could end up in this kind of mess, you don't know very much. You see, as we move forward among the unreached people, the Muslims, and enemy strongholds, Satan is going to release all hell against us. Without that humility and awe, the love which breaks us, and the repentance that must come, Christianity is nothing.

If you're going to win people to be co-laborers, it won't be because of your great knowledge of discipleship, your great theological ability, your cleverness, or your education. If you're going to disciple people, it will happen because you're a humble, broken servant of Jesus Christ who is willing to take the hard road of humility, even when you don't fully understand it.

15

Winning by Losing

The importance of giving up rights

by Loren Cunningham

Loren Cunningham, Founder and International Director of Youth With A Mission, is the author of Is That Really You, God?, Winning, God's Way, *and* Daring to Live on the Edge.

Some years ago, my young bride and I were driving night and day across the United States in our VW van. Just after dawn one morning, I gave Darlene the wheel and crawled into the back to take a nap. We were traveling through southern Arizona on our way to Tucson.

I woke to the lurching of our van as it began rolling over and over. A few seconds later, I found myself thrown out of the vehicle. The dust was still flying as I looked around me. The VW lay on its side—totaled. Everything we owned was scattered on the desert. Then I panicked. Where was my wife? I found her a few yards away, her head bashed in, her eyes rolled back, and she wasn't even trying to breathe.

As I sat there in despair, cradling her battered head, God spoke to me. He asked, "Loren, are you willing to serve Me?"

I thought and replied, "Yes, Lord. I have nothing left but You."

Until that moment, I hadn't realized that I truly didn't own anything. We speak of *my* family, *my* house, *my* ministry, *my* car, *my* reputation, but we can lose them all within seconds. All of these things are given to us by God for a time, to use for His glory.

As soon as I said, "Yes, Lord, I'll serve You," God spoke a second time. He told me to pray for Darlene. It hadn't occurred to me to pray for her; I thought she was already dead. As I prayed, she began to breathe and fight for life. A Mexican man found us and went for help. An hour later, we were in an ambulance on the long trip to the hospital. She was still unconscious, but God spoke a third time, telling me that my wife would be okay.

Darlene recovered, and we have enjoyed over 25 years together

since that day in the desert. But I have never forgotten my promise
to the Lord to serve Him. Giving up our right to the people and
things God has given us is at the very core of Christian discipleship.

We have rights as individuals. The Bible says that every good
and perfect gift comes down from the Father (James 1:17). God gave
us the right to a family. God gave us the right to possessions, the
right to freedom, the right to our country, and the right to other
basic blessings. All of these things are good.

The Hindus say that the material world is evil, while the Buddhists say that only in turning away from the things of this world
will we achieve reality. Yet God looked at the earth He created and
said, "It is good." And God looks at us and the rights He has given
us and says, "It is good."

Then why is He asking us to give up those rights? Because He
wants to give us greater things. This is a rule of God's Kingdom:
Give up something good and receive something greater. Give up
your rights and you'll receive greater privileges with God.

God gives us the right to own possessions. God underscored the
right to personal property in the Ten Commandments. But God
wants us to open our hands rather than tightly clench our fists
around what we own. He says we can't be a servant to money and
a servant to Him at the same time. He gives us the right to own
things, and then asks us to freely give back to Him that with which
He has blessed us.

When we give up the right to spend our money as we want and
are able to say to God, "Tell me what *You* want. All I have is Yours.
What do You want me to give back to You?" then we will see God
as our provider. Only then will we have the excitement of seeing
Him do the miraculous to meet our needs.

We've been given other rights, too. We were born to our particular parents, raised in a certain neighborhood, and brought up to
believe certain things. Our moms prepared food in a particular
way, and those dishes probably are our favorite foods to this day.
Whether we are American, Filipino, or Swiss, or grew up in Seattle
or Shanghai, these things are part of what makes us who we are.

When we need something to wear, we go out and buy what we
like. That probably will be influenced by the way others we admire
dress themselves. It could be an outfit like the one we've seen
everyone else wearing at school, or if we live in a Malaysian village,
it could be a certain way to tie hand-dyed sarongs. Whatever it is,
we're happier and feel best when we dress a certain way, eat certain

foods, live in a certain kind of house, and raise our children to do the things that are important to us.

Even our choice of which church to attend is influenced by our background, our choices, our likes and dislikes, and our experiences. We may like to worship in a plain building with happy, informal singing and preaching. We may like stained glass windows and a soaring pipe organ. These are all parts of our culture, our heritage, our denomination, our families, and our upbringing.

Furthermore, we have the right to be an American (or an Australian, Brazilian, or Russian). We have the right to enjoy our own culture and country. We have the right to belong to a certain church and to other groups that express what we believe is important. We have a right to live and to talk and to eat.

But if everyone exercises their rights to the exclusion of God's plans, a tragedy of cataclysmic proportions will occur. Millions of people will live their lives in guilt and despair, and will die to face judgment for their sins eternally in hell. There are more than 2.7 billion people who have never heard the Gospel. More than 12,000 unreached people groups wait for a Christian witness.

All we have to do to seal the fate of these millions is to stay where we are, in comfortable surroundings, eating the food we like, going to the church we enjoy, wearing clothes suited to us, staying with friends who talk about what we like to talk about, and shutting our ears to God's cry, "Whom shall I send? And who will go for us?"

Jesus gave us the supreme example of giving up everything for a greater goal. Philippians chapter two says He didn't count equality with God a thing to be grasped, but emptied Himself, taking the form of a bond-servant—a slave. Slaves have no rights, and Jesus became a slave for our sakes:

- He gave up the right to be with His Father.
- He gave up the right to a home, saying that while the birds have nests and the foxes have dens, He didn't have a place to lay His head.
- He gave up the right to money. He had to borrow a coin from someone for a sermon illustration.
- He gave up the right to marriage and His reputation. As far as most people were concerned, He was an illegitimate baby, raised in a town that was scorned. The ultimate slur to His reputation came when He, the Son of God, was called a devil by the religious experts of His time. But Jesus went further.

- He gave up the right to life itself, becoming obedient to death on a cross. For what purpose? So that God might exalt Him, give Him a name above every other name, that at His name every knee should bow. But there's another reason: Jesus was showing us how to live our lives. He was showing us how to win over the devil, which is the greatest job ever given to us—taking the earth from Satan and winning it back for God. Jesus was showing us that the only way to win is to lose; the only way to conquer is to submit.

Jesus wants us to follow Him, losing our rights and gaining the world. Only by taking Jesus' example into every part of our lives will we be able to win in life.

He spelled it out for us in Mark 8:34-35: "If anyone would come after me, he must deny himself and take up his cross and follow me. For whoever wants to save his life will lose it, but whoever loses his life for me and for the gospel will save it."

The choice is ours. We can hold onto our rights, remain in mediocrity, and miss out on God's greater purposes for us. Or we can give them freely back to Him for the greatest privilege of all—winning this world for the Kingdom of God.

16

Trial by Team

How to build good team relationships

by Dave Hicks

*Dave Hicks, North America Director of Operation Mobilisation, spent five years in India working with teams of young adults. He learned the art of team relationships leading hundreds of short-termers on the ministry ship m/v **Logos**.*

The number one problem in missionary work today is broken, strained relationships. Someone said, "To live above with the saints we love—oh, that will be glory. But to live below with the saints we know can be a different story." The number of career missionaries who return home after one term or less and never go out again because of shattered relationships is astounding.

It shouldn't surprise us that relationships are such a battleground, because the only thing that will last for eternity is our relationship with God and our relationships with one another. Nothing else will endure. None of our mission organizations, church buildings, houses, cars, bank accounts, or educational degrees will survive the grave.

When our relationships are strong, enormous resources are released to accomplish the work of God. When relationships are strained, the energy of the Holy Spirit working through us is drained away. It makes sense, therefore, that Satan's strategy is to undermine relationships among believers, especially those intent on serving Christ.

All of us have experienced relationship problems that distract us from Christian service. It's easy for us to become so focused on a poor relationship, so hurt by it, so perplexed about how to resolve it, that we become sidetracked. Today the Church of Jesus Christ is often tragically diverted from the task of communicating the Gospel because of broken relationships.

In John 17, Jesus prays for the unity of His disciples and "those who will believe in me through their message." That's us! Jesus prays, "May they be brought to complete unity to let the world know that you sent me and have loved them even as you have loved me" (John 17:23).

Our practical unity with other believers is the first evangelistic method we have. Jesus says our unity lets the world know that the Father sent Him and that God loves us. That is the very heart of the Gospel message.

As we move across cultural barriers to share God's love, the foundation of all our communication (whether it be acts of compassion, friendship, behind-the-scenes practical service, or literature distribution) is a godly quality of relationships between us and our co-workers.

Because right relationships undergird all ministries, we must give highest priority to resolving relationship problems on a mission team. I remember serving with a short-term team in West Bengal. As the only foreigner on a team of eight Indians, my job was to lead the team's Bible study program and to drive a large truck, which was our mobile evangelistic base and home.

One day, just before driving out to a crowded market to preach, distribute Scriptures, and do personal work, tempers on the team flared. Our Indian team leader called us all together and said that we couldn't go out to evangelize until we got right with each other. Right there in the back of the truck, we confessed our sins, forgave each other, and prayed together. Later that afternoon, we weren't surprised to experience unusual interest and responsiveness among the Hindu villagers.

One benefit of short-term service is to see the Bible come alive in new ways as you get into situations where God must act to keep you out of deep trouble. The Bible is full of practical instructions on resolving and keeping relationships right. I've found three basic principles helpful in learning to live together.

Let Love Cover

In the rubs and scrapes of everyday life—let alone in missionary service—we must know the reality of allowing God's love to cover our interaction with others. I lived for five-and-a-half years on the mission ship *Logos* with 130 others from 25 nations. If we'd taken up each offense and misunderstanding with one another, we never would have accomplished anything. Love is like the oil that covers the moving parts in the main diesel engine which propels the ship forward. Without oil, the engine overheats and locks up. However, there are situations where love doesn't cover, but actually causes us to *uncover* that which is sinful and wrong.

Seek Forgiveness

Take the initiative to go and ask for forgiveness. In Matthew 5:23 and 24, Jesus says, "If you are offering your gift at the altar and there remember that your brother has something against you, leave your gift there in front of the altar. First go and be reconciled to your brother; then come and offer your gift." With God, reconciliation has a higher priority than worship, because true worship can't occur when relationships aren't right.

If you're aware that your brother has something against you, one of two things must be true. Either you've done something against him, or he thinks you have. In either case, the next move is yours, not his. Go and be reconciled with him.

The Church is full of offended people waiting for others to make the first move. Jesus says that it's your move if you're aware the other person is hurt. If you're the offender, you need to go immediately, ask forgiveness, and make full restitution. Even if it seems that the other party is more at fault, take full responsibility for your own wrong.

Carefully Confront

Take the initiative to go when you're aware of sin in the life of another believer. "If your brother sins against you, go and show him his fault, just between the two of you" (Matt. 18:15).

What does Jesus say here? "If your brother sins against you, go and *tell* a lot of people about it"? That's not what it says, but that's what we usually do, isn't it? We go and tell other people. "Do you know what I saw John do the other night?" or "You know, I don't really know exactly how to approach this person. I wonder if I can get some advice from you." And when we go to other people, we immediately erode the potential for that person to come back, to confess, and to be restored, because as the news spreads, the stakes get higher. The higher the stakes, the harder it is for the offender to repent.

The whole purpose of Matthew 18:15-17 is to help sinners confess their sins and experience restoration. The purpose of loving confrontation is not to make life hard for them, embarrass them, or hurt them. It's to bring healing and reconciliation.

"If your brother sins against you, go and show him his fault, just between the two of you." Very explicit, isn't it? Don't tell him in front of the other team members, because the approach is so important. Do it privately. Do everything possible to make it as easy as possible for that person to admit the wrong, to ask forgiveness, and to be restored to fellowship with the Lord and with you. If you go and say, "You miserable sinner; I don't understand how you could ever do something as terrible as this," you haven't created an atmosphere in which that person can easily acknowledge the sin and confess it. Go in humility.

Don't start off by accusing the person. Because you don't have the full story, say, "You know, the other night I noticed you in this situation. Would you tell me what was happening there?" When you ask questions, it's much less threatening.

I don't like to confront others. If you like to go to people and point out their sins, you have a problem. But the Word of God doesn't say, "If you feel like going, go." It doesn't say, "If you think it's a good idea, go." It says "Go." That's a command.

In Matthew 18, Jesus gives us a basic set of steps for seeking reconciliation. In verse 16, we read, "But if he will not listen, take one or two others along, so that every matter may be established by the testimony of two or three witnesses." If the person refuses to listen, or says that what you're saying isn't true, then take one or two others along.

On your mission team, this would be the time to bring the team leader into the situation, unless the team leader is the one you're confronting. If it's the team leader, then you need to take another mature team member with you.

You need to go first yourself, then with one or two others, and then to the spiritual authorities supervising your team if the situation is still unresolved.

Let love cover. Ask for forgiveness. Go and confront compassionately. As you serve Christ, these three principles, when applied to the inevitable struggle of interpersonal relationships, can produce a unity that will let the world know that the Father sent Jesus and has loved you even as He has loved Jesus. Pack these principles in your suitcase between your socks and towel, because you'll need them.

17

Follow the Leader

How to serve those in charge

by Stephen T. Hoke

Stephen T. Hoke spent 15 years growing up in Japan, and is now training the next generation of World Christians for cross-cultural ministry as Vice-President for Training at Church Resource Ministries.

When Ray went overseas for further education and ministry, he never anticipated the traumatic events to follow. He volunteered for a leadership role soon after arriving overseas at the Christian school where he was studying. His position linked him to an older adult experienced in the language, the culture, and the specifics of the ministry.

But Ray didn't take the time to listen to advice or come under the spiritual counsel of his leader. He wanted to begin new ministries, form gospel teams, and change the world—not spend his time listening to advice.

He initiated projects without informing his leaders, and sometimes even deceived those who asked questions. Before long, Ray had isolated himself from his team and leaders. He was eventually dismissed and had to leave the country because he hadn't followed their advice in filing properly for visas and alien registration.

Ray's story is an extreme, but true, one. All too many short-term workers neglect building relationships with their leaders.

Relating well with the leaders on your short term will demand change on your part. Get ready, because getting to know and work with your leaders will tug you and stretch you in directions you never imagined.

Follow

Ask yourself, "How can I best serve the leaders God has given me?" You may relate with your leaders in all kinds of ways, but the working relationship is different. Quickly learn how best to work with your leaders. How do they want you to keep them informed? If you have a question, how would you proceed? How often do they want you to meet with them? What kind of indicators show them you're accomplishing your task?

Look for ways to support their ministry. Be willing to submit to their advice and counsel.

Accept

Accept your leaders rather than trying to fight them or change them. Be prepared for disappointment. Mission leaders are ordinary disciples, seeking to grow in Christ themselves.

I've worked under at least four kinds of leaders: some have been timid, others tired, many traditional, and some touchy. Learn to respect the position of each type of leader, even if you disagree with the person. Look for ways to affirm; don't criticize and intimidate.

Learn

Get to know those you're following. As you develop a personal relationship with your leaders, you'll be better equipped to understand why they do what they do.

Observe their ministry closely. As you do, remember Romans 13:1 and Hebrews 13:17. Seeing your leaders as divinely appointed mentors or disciplers will free you to learn from and with them as you minister side by side.

When Sam went to Africa, he was eager to apply his Christian education degree and make an impact in Kenya. He wisely chose to be discipled by an itinerant Kenyan evangelist for the first two years. The intimate exposure afforded by traveling and working together helped Sam learn how to weave a strong fabric of relationships with national Christians, pastors, and church leaders. It was out of these interwoven relationships that Sam was able to build a continent-wide ministry in leadership development over the course of the next five years.

Looking back, Sam reflects, "I learned a lot of hard lessons I would never have learned had I not chosen to submit myself to my leader."

Look for your leaders' strengths in ministry. How do they relate to national pastors? How do they engage in natural evangelism? How do they plan? How do they balance ministry demands with family life? When you don't understand why they do what they do, ask. Few leaders feel comfortable in demanding time with short-term workers, but most are flattered when asked for the time for conversation and counsel.

Spend time getting to know them by asking some of the following questions:

- Why did you get involved in Christian ministry?
- What helped and hindered you the most as you started out?
- What are some of the greatest lessons you've learned?
- What would you do differently if you could live your life over?
- What were your greatest mistakes? Your most fulfilling accomplishments?
- What aspect of your ministry has been most enjoyable?

Initiate

Most leaders pray for motivated, responsible co-workers. They're looking for people who will jump in with fresh ideas and follow them through to completion. If you understand the context in which you're working and the parameters of the task, offer suggestions and be available when work needs to be done.

Pray

Make it a priority to pray daily and specifically for each of the people serving you as leaders. Bathe your relationship in prayer, committing the rough spots to the Lord. Let their personal pain and triumph drive you to your knees.

Work zealously at following your leader. Give it your best shot. Paul was wholehearted and zealous in *all* his work for God. *Zeal* refers to something within that "boils up"—the enthusiasm that irresistibly bubbles up in the heart.

Pray that God's Spirit will keep you at that boiling point in your desire to build lasting relationships with your leaders during your short-term mission.

18

Allies

Building relationships with missionaries

by Stephen T. Hoke

Stephen T. Hoke spent 15 years growing up in Japan, and is now training the next generation of World Christians for cross-cultural ministry as Vice-President for Training at Church Resource Ministries.

Get ready for a real surprise! You'll meet few stereotypical missionaries in your short term overseas. You will meet some heroes and heroines of faith. You'll meet people who display the same embarrassingly human foibles you do. They are men and women who are living out kingdom values and lifestyles in stark contrast to "the lifestyles of the rich and famous."

How can you best relate to this group of God's people about whom libraries of biographies and case studies have been written? The following tips will help you traverse the missions mine field and establish contact with your trusted allies in the battle.

Study the Missionary Subculture

Just as you've studied the host culture and country to which you're going, carve out time to get to know the subculture of missionaries living overseas. Just like your host culture, the expatriate missionary community has a social structure with its own leaders, folkways, and strange customs. It is not as formidable as a foreign culture often is, because many of the artifacts and behaviors are familiar to you. But there are a number of idiosyncracies you may want to be aware of before you trip over them. For example, missionaries I've met in Japan don't drink, smoke, or dance, but on their vacations, they love to play Rook until all hours of the night.

Make the effort to learn when the mission movement entered a particular region, and discover who is who and who does what. It will inform your first impressions and deepen your discernment of who to approach when you need assistance.

Invest Time Building Relationships

Getting to know busy missionaries takes time. Look for those natural breaks in their schedules to ask questions, and listen to their oral histories of battles and victories. And take advantage of their hospitality. Observe their family life over meals together. Spend time with their children and spouses. Be willing to fit into their vacations, holidays, and family celebrations. Show up for the days of prayer, potlucks, and Friday night fellowships. Sharing Christmas, Thanksgiving, and Easter celebrations among missionary communities overseas will provide rich Christian fellowship. Fellowship under fire is the sweetest in the world.

Missionaries also know how to have fun. Skin diving in the Philippines, climbing Kilimanjaro or Mt. Fuji, eating in Hong Kong or Singapore, or singing in Harare or Sao Paulo are some of the cross-cultural memories you can store away while overseas.

Practice Your Serve

One way to determine your effectiveness on the mission field is to ask yourself, "Am I a burden or a blessing to those with whom I work?" In a relational, team-oriented ministry, your contribution can easily be determined by evaluating your service. Take the initiative. Most needs are obvious: setting up the room, passing out literature, carrying the luggage, typing a letter, clearing the tables, taking care of crying children. When you see a need, meet it.

Be a Barnabas

Quite possibly the most significant role you can play in your first short-term assignment is that of being a spiritual cheerleader to other players desperately in need of rest and recuperation. Just as first-century Barnabas played a role of tremendous significance in the life of the Early Church by encouraging Paul and John Mark, so you, too, can have an impact on the lives of countless missionary co-workers by your positive praise and consistent affirmation.

Marti arrived on the field in early June, when missionary moods were at a low ebb. In spite of budget cuts and dismal evangelistic response, Marti continued to cheer others on with simple words of exhortation to stick with it, to keep expecting a miracle, and to trust the Lord. By the mid-August Field Conference, a core of missionaries had gained renewed hope and vision for the year ahead. Shortly before Marti left for home after only six months, the chairman of the field council took her aside. "Marti," he said quietly, "I want to thank you for your loving encouragement and the impact you have had on the spirit of our entire mission family."

Pray For and With Missionaries

On the mission field, prayer becomes your lifeline. The stronger and wider it is, the more strength you can draw for the struggle. Talking to God about your missionaries will do more to change them than any amount of talking you do with them.

From my personal experience of praying with a missionary on a weekly basis, I could tell he knew the needs of his staff intimately. He also knew the names of inquiring Japanese students open to the Gospel. Over the course of three years, praying with Johnny at our weekly meetings expanded my entire perspective on what prayer was all about.

Short-term mission work is essentially teamwork. Only when we work as partners can we accomplish our global task.

19

No Longer Strangers

Building relationships with nationals

by Stephen T. Hoke

Stephen T. Hoke spent 15 years growing up in Japan, and is now training the next generation of World Christians for cross-cultural ministry as Vice-President for Training at Church Resource Ministries.

"East is east, and west is west, and never the twain shall meet." Sometimes it seems that in relationships between missionaries and nationals, Rudyard Kipling was right. The gap between cultures seems uncrossable. The differences between cultures outweigh the similarities.

After two months in Brazil, Joyce wrote in her diary: "It's hard for me to believe that people who look so alike on the outside can be and think so differently on the inside. Even though we are both Christians, we perceive reality from opposite sides of the sea."

Can missionaries get to the point where they are no longer strangers in a foreign country? Can cultural barriers be broken down sufficiently to model that international community of faith we all espouse? The following practical guidelines for building relationships with nationals in the host country can guide you in "taking off masks" and "tearing down walls."

Get Involved

Many ministry opportunities are missed by short-termers because their attitude is that of ministering to, not ministering among or with. In Matthew 20:20-28, Jesus rebuked His disciples for the very same attitude of subtle superiority.

Resist the impulse to pull away and spend time mainly with other missionaries or expatriates. Stories of the dangers of culture shock, the stress of learning the language, and the loneliness of cross-cultural careers abound. Fear of failing or offending might cause you to become overly sensitive, tentative, never venturing forth or initiating friendship.

But it need not be that way. Two-year relief worker Celia wrote:

"The most fulfilling part of my entire time in Africa was the friendships that grew with my Somali co-workers. Not all of them were Christians, but as we saw health emerge from the hell around us, our experiences bonded us together for life."

Learning the language and studying the culture are two steps that can prepare you to know people personally. Don't stop there. Attempt to develop friendships with different types of people, from taxi drivers to night watchmen, from secretaries to village midwives. Talk to people across the spectrum of social roles and levels in society. Attend local churches. Observe regional celebrations. Try relaxing the way local people relax—walking, talking under the trees, or playing soccer.

Linguists Tom and Betty Brewster highly recommend "bonding" with your host culture by living in the home of a local family for the first week or more after arriving overseas. This exposure will develop a personal, social, cultural, and spiritual bond between you and your hosts unlike anything you can develop in classes or by reading a book. Bonding comes by rubbing life on life.

Get Your Information Straight

Be aware that friendships in other cultures often do not mean exactly what we think they might. What we call *friend*, other cultures might call *acquaintance*. Friendship for them involves a commitment of time and self-sacrifice to a degree many Westerners do not understand and for which they're unprepared. At first, greetings will be sincere and hospitality genuine. But many cultures maintain a protective distance.

All the information you will need to close the gap is readily available. But you'll have to ask those around you. Spend time viewing life from the perspective of the nationals. Learn to ask good questions of your national co-workers and friends. Larry and Rob ended each workday of their six months in Thailand eating a leisurely dinner and talking with Thai co-workers in the refugee camps. Relationships of trust emerged as fear and ignorance were replaced by knowledge and empathy gained through nightly story telling and visits in each other's homes.

Get Ready to Break Down Barriers

Your information gathering will reveal some barriers. Try to identify the most significant barriers. In Asia, it may be subtleties of culture; in Africa, their fear of being assimilated by the West; in Latin America, the North-South ideological debate. Prayer will sensitize you to interpersonal issues to be resolved.

Work to remove or tear down those barriers over which you have some control or influence. Focus on similarities between people and culture; don't highlight the differences. Find a reliable sponsor in your new culture who is willing to give you honest and direct feedback on your language and behavior. Let that person serve as both a model and teacher to you in the nuances of cultural differences and folkways.

Church history is packed with emotionally gripping accounts of western missionaries who got involved, sought information, and broke all sorts of cultural barriers. They developed life-transforming relationships with national Christians in other cultures. Contemporary Christian missions should be an ongoing testimony to the truth of the apostle Paul's declaration, "You are no longer foreigners...but fellow citizens with God's people and members of God's household" (Eph. 2:19).

20

God's Gift Arrived First

Learning through cultural differences

by Miriam Adeney

Miriam Adeney is author of four books, Associate Professor at Seattle Pacific University, and Adjunct Professor at Regent College. She worked several years in the Philippines; has ministered in Micronesia, East Asia, Latin America, West Africa, and Russia; and is writing a book on ministry to Muslim women.

"Lord," Jojo began, "we thank You so much for sending Ron and Linda to us."

While the bamboo trees creaked like doors on rusty hinges, nineteen Filipinos and three foreigners sat in an open shed, praying. Tonight we were concentrating on each other's needs.

"...for their careful Bible teaching, their beautiful personal lives, their warm home, their enthusiasm and energy in serving You." Ron, Linda, and I were the only foreigners on the staff.

"And Lord," Jojo continued, "we beg You to deliver them from tension."

I was a little surprised. Tension? In their capable, efficient ministry? Well, yes, I suppose I'd seen them tense when they were weak from hepatitis, or tired of wading around dead rats floating through the flooded market, or busy planning week-long conferences. Yes, maybe they could relax a little more.

A gecko slithered down the roof beam. The prayers murmured on. Then I heard Arturo praying for me.

"...and, our Father, we ask You to deliver her from tension."

Tension, again? What was this all about? Were we foreigners so much more tense than everybody else?

As a matter of fact, yes. We like efficiency so much that we got uptight with lagging schedules. The Filipinos had learned to adjust, because their land is one where natural or political typhoons could demolish any system. As a result, peace characterized non-Christian Filipinos more than it did many of us missionaries.

Hadn't we been sent out to help? Yet we were discovering that the recipients of our generosity were, in ways, superior to us.

God's Gift in Cultures

When I looked around at my Filipino neighbors, I saw strong families. Hospitality. Lots of time lavished on children. Enduring loyalties. The ability to live graciously on little money. A heritage of economic freedom for women. Creativity in music. Sauces that deliciously extended a little meat to many people. Skill in the art of relaxation. The ability to positively enjoy being with a large number of people continuously.

Since every good gift comes from above, and since all wisdom and knowledge come from Jesus Christ, these beautiful qualities of the Filipino culture are gifts from God. It seems that just as our Creator delights in a variety of colors and smells, just as He has ordained an amazing spectrum of cultures, He has programmed into people the capacity to make culture to enrich His world.

Early Christians learned to accept different cultures. When they preached to the Jews, their framework was the law of Moses and the prophets. But when their audience was pagan, they dropped that emphasis and talked about how God provides for physical and spiritual needs, and how God is stronger than idols.

Peter learned to accept all peoples, including their "repulsive" food. Paul learned to be all things to all men. Timothy was circumcised; Titus wasn't. Yet both were Paul's key men. The Epistles show that churches from different cultural backgrounds had different kinds of problems. So when leaders in the mother church in Jerusalem set standards, they decided not to ask new Christians in other cultures to conform to their ways, since there was "no distinction between us and them" (Acts 15:9).

On the other hand, people who form cultures are made in God's image, but they're also sinners. The cultures we've developed contain good qualities but also exploitative and immoral ones. That's why the Bible says we shouldn't love the world or be conformed to it, but be transformed by God's spirit.

We aren't to be conformists to any culture. Neither are we to be dropouts. Rather, both at home and abroad, we must be creatively different, people of conviction in the middle of the mass, the salt of the earth.

This robust theology of culture gives us a good foundation for appreciating our national brothers' and sisters' strengths, as well as their weaknesses.

Get Involved

No list of hints can guide you through what you'll face. The simple solution is to spend time with the local people as much as possible. If you can, live with a national family, especially during the first couple of months. Use public transportation whenever possible. (Take sensible precautions: find out where you should travel and if you should go only during daylight or only with a group.) Be aware of local judgments on specific American material goods, and live simply. Learn to like their music, sports, games, and conversational styles. Get your news from local media. Expose yourself to regular spiritual nurture and direction from Christians in the culture. Learn to like the culture's values. Have a disciplined program for learning the language; there's no better way to begin sharing their thoughts.

Find some of your closest friends from among members of that culture. Don't turn to an American every time you have a problem. If you do that, you'll never really need the local people, and they'll always remain a "project." Cultivate enough loneliness so that you turn to a local person as a fellow human being. Reciprocal need is one of the ingredients of friendship.

Various regions have various expectations for foreigners' adaptation. You may choose to be different because of ethical conviction, to affirm your own roots, or because of personal taste. After all, maybe you were different even in the United States. But remember, for every missionary who overadapts, 99 don't go far enough.

Sin is present in other cultures, but it's in ours, too. So are God's gifts. Share them on your short term. Maybe you have something to teach about individual responsibility. Maybe you have something to learn about being delivered from tension.

Ways to Relate

Here are some suggestions to help you smooth your relationships with the nationals you meet:

1. Age. Show respect for older people. Stand up and be prepared to give an appropriate greeting—a nod, a handshake, a bow, or whatever the specific culture expects. When circulating in a group, always take time to talk with older people.

2. Hierarchy. Show respect for community leaders, too. Learn a few appropriate status titles (elder brother, engineer, mayor, and nurse, for instance), and use them when you address these people. In general, avoid calling people simply by their first names. Listen, and ask people what's courteous.

3. Sex. Avoid being alone with or talking at length with someone of the opposite sex, especially if this isn't the custom. Dress modestly, whatever that means locally. Again, don't be afraid to ask.

4. Formality. If you have a position of importance (teacher, for example), polish your shoes and wear clothing in a way that reflects honor onto your students. I keep in mind a Filipino friend's mother who drilled into her, "No matter how poor you are, always wear perfume."

5. Conversation style. Americans tend to talk too much, so be sensitive to whether your new friends might like to express themselves, or whether they want to listen to you. Some people groups communicate through hints and metaphors rather than frankness; some, through satirical repartee and overstatements; some, through stories. As a rule, well-told stories will be appreciated, including stories of your life in Christ. Polish some of these anecdotes before you go.

6. Time. Be flexible, not uptight. Go with the flow of the culture and ministry in which you're involved.

7. Groups. Most peoples are more rooted in groups than we are, so don't treat a friend as an isolated individual. Ask about his or her family and friends, and try to get to know them. Learn to tolerate a crowd. Likewise, talk positively about your family, and be ready to show photos. (Keep in mind that many foreigners can't understand your testimony if you say negative things about your family.)

8. Anger. In many Asian cultures, and in some tribal ones, losing your temper is about the greatest sin possible. Keep quiet. Defuse explosive emotions in your journal or in prayer.

9. Photos. Be sure you don't offend people by taking photos of what they consider their private space or of what they consider to be a negative aspect of their country.

10. Beggars. Philosophies differ and countries differ, but consider the example of one short-termer in Haiti. Every morning, she tore up a loaf of bread and filled her large purse with the pieces. Throughout the day, as she was confronted by beggars, she handed out bread. Every night, she came home with an empty purse, but with the blessings of people who had been truly hungry.

21

Taking Marriage Overseas

Helping the relationship all the way

by Dan and Bonnie Porter

Dan and Bonnie Porter have been married 23 years. Dan is Church Planting Team Leader for Mission to the World's new work in Milan, Italy for the Presbyterian Church in America. Bonnie is mother to their three sons and is a free-lance writer.

We took ten teenagers to Mexico for two weeks and lived to tell about it. In a short time, we experienced practically the whole gamut of marital pressures. Lack of privacy. Confusion over roles. No time alone as a couple. Traveling separately.

We know many other couples who have also been short-termers. Though our situation differed, our responses were the same; it was one of the greatest experiences of our lives.

Deciding to Go

Different things motivate different people. It's important that both of you identify your goals and reasons for going.

Maybe your mate just wants to experience a foreign culture. Maybe you desire to use your college French. Get your motives out in the open. Talk about them.

We discovered that one of us had a strong desire simply to expand our family's horizons. But we both saw the trip as an opportunity to investigate a long-term assignment.

Plan a candlelight dinner or a weekend retreat with an agenda. Discuss motives for wanting to go; goals that you each want to make; what it would take for each of you to know God wants you to go; feelings you have about the privacy, competition, and other issues raised below. Pray together about what you've discussed.

Going as a "Married Single"

One couple we know had a hard time overseas because their group of five all lived in one hut with only a sheet between them and the singles.

"Anticipating what it would be like really worked for us," said another couple. "We knew we would be the only couple on the team. We expected to be separated most of the time."

An attitude of flexibility is the best preparation for functional singleness. It will enable you to cope with:

- little or no privacy;
- "distance" created by task-related roles;
- finding your niche (especially wife's);
- functioning separately, not as a couple.

Competing on the Go

If there is a tendency to compete in your relationship, expect it to surface overseas. So one couple suggests: "Go as a team, giving mutual support."

During our summer project, Bonnie quickly renewed her language comprehension while Dan struggled with the basics. The threat was there: humiliation and avoidance. But Dan's effort to communicate paid off. It changed his perspective on the new culture and about himself.

A couple returning from a two-year term explained that their marriage and ministry "tended to get mixed up together." The wife said, "We worked so closely together that my husband was my boss." Solution? "We scheduled in some relaxation time, even separate activities."

Going With Priorities

Ministry time can easily absorb all marriage time. Amid all the changes and activities overseas, your spouse can quickly become a stranger. It's up to you whether you pull together or let stress drive you apart. Determine before you go to make your marriage a high priority.

Each couple needs to work at building a strong and enduring marriage—upon biblical principles. This will involve sacrifice and creativity. If you want to grow together as a couple, expect to give up some group activities or special events to spend time together. Plan to study Scripture together regularly. Set aside time to pray as a family. Read through at least one book together, such as *To Understand Each Other* by Paul Tournier. Try to plan a date night at least once a week to get alone and talk.

Other issues include marital communication, long-term effects on finances and careers, relatives' opinions, language aptitude, and taking children overseas.

Schedule a weekend retreat shortly after you come back. You'll need the time together to process the experience. If you've each kept a journal, use them as springboards for discussion.

You may find yourselves uncovering unexpected areas of growth in your relationship. We can truthfully say that our times spent overseas have added a dimension to our marriage which we would not trade for anything in the world.

22

Taking the Kids

A survival guide for families on the field

by Joyce Bowers

Joyce Bowers and her husband Louis spent 11 years as educational missionaries to Liberia, West Africa. Their two daughters were born and spent their early years there.

Soon after we arrived in Liberia, my three-year-old daughter asked for a story at bedtime. She often asked for stories, but on this night, I was too tired to think of a plot. Feeling uncreative, I began, "I know a little girl who eats Cheerios..." and described a day in the life she'd just left in America. She squealed with delight and jumped to correct me. "Cornflakes!" she said.

Afterward, my daughter asked for more installments of the story. As time went on, I talked about life in Liberia, and included her Ghanian, Liberian, and German playmates in the story.

It took a lot of time to help our daughter adjust to life overseas. That's one reason relatively few families with children undertake short-term assignments. Uprooting, moving, and adjusting to a different culture and lifestyle take huge investments of time and energy for a family. Assignments that last less than one year may be too short. Service overseas costs a lot, but it pays off, too. The rewards of family enrichment last a lifetime.

If you have children older than eight or nine, the whole family should make the decision to go. It's unwise to burden a very young child with an adult decision, but it's a recipe for disaster to forcefully uproot a child, especially a teenager, against his or her will. If the process of information gathering along with your own growing enthusiasm doesn't engage the interest and willingness of a child, it may be better to alter plans. On the other hand, an excited, informed, and prepared child may receive lifelong benefits from the cross-cultural experience.

Preparation

If there's one thing that spells the difference between a successful adjustment to overseas living and a family disaster, it's preparation. Make it a family project to learn about the history and geography of the country, and about the customs of the people with whom you'll share your life.

Finding out the specifics of your living arrangements is more critical for families with children than for adults without children. What kind of house might you live in? What variety of food can you buy? How do you shop for it? Can you drink the water? How will you wash and dry diapers? How about medical care? Is public transportation available? What kind? Are there telephones? Do they work? Is mail service reliable? What should you bring and what should you purchase locally?

In some places, whether or not to hire a household helper is an important concern. Shopping can take half the day, and cooking the other half. But having a helper who speaks a language you don't share and who finds your way of doing things incomprehensible may bring as much bane as blessing. On the other hand, "inheriting" well-trained household help or baby sitters from other expatriates can lead to increased comfort with the local situation as well as, in many cases, warm and strong friendships with your worker and his or her family.

If your children will attend school, be sure to investigate what education is available. Like long-term missionaries, you may have to decide among local, international, or missionary schools; home teaching; and other alternatives. Don't assume that because a school is there it will accept your child, especially midyear; some schools have waiting lists. Also, find out how your child will get to and from school, and whether you need to bring supplemental books from home.

Another vital element in preparation is developing cross-cultural awareness and skills. Children easily learn cross-cultural sensitivities, but if they're living in a mono-cultural context, they must be taught. Link Care Foundation (Attn: Ron McLain, 1734 W. Shaw Ave., Fresno, CA 93711) has developed an excellent workbook entitled *Rookies*, which gives specific family activities designed to prepare children for cross-cultural living.

Another excellent resource for anyone considering or preparing for service in another culture is Ted Ward's *Living Overseas: A Book of Preparations*. Ward gives advice on developing the kind of insight that makes for a successful experience, including such nitty-gritty issues as how to handle bargaining and beggars, and lists excellent resources for further information.

Making the Transition

As you leave your family's familiar surroundings, anticipate a process of grief. To a child, even six months seems like forever. Talk about this as a family. Involve children in decisions about which of their possessions go with you and which stay home. Goodbye parties and rituals give a sense of closure.

While in transition, preserve as much routine and predictability as possible. Conduct a daily orientation session, perhaps at breakfast. Go over the events of the day in the context of where you have come from and where you are going. Even if the child is too young to understand the details, he or she will have the comfort and security of knowing that things are happening with some degree of predictability.

Young children enjoy bedtime conversations. You might keep handy a small photo album of familiar people and surroundings to provide comfort, along with favorite security blankets, toys, or other cherished objects. And the more you can relax and enjoy the adventure, the easier the transition will be for your children.

Living in a New Setting

Overseas, your family time will probably increase. Enjoy it. Maintain family traditions. Invite neighbors to join you for a game night, an unheard-of pleasure in our overscheduled society. As you begin to settle down, and as the magnitude of the change sinks in, expect young children to regress temporarily, possibly wetting the bed, having problems sleeping, getting sick more often, or being cranky or irritable more often. As an antidote, spend time giving "TLC," cuddling, stroking (physically and psychologically), and talking about what was left behind and what is facing them now. It takes an enormous investment of time and energy in the first four to six months to enable a family to adjust to a new culture.

Children don't need to be protected from contact with nationals. In fact, children can become one of the best bridges to relationships in your new setting. On the other hand, respect a child's own personality and individual pace. Older children can learn to use public transit, bargain with peddlers, and become quite independent and well-integrated into the host culture. They often adapt more easily than parents if given the chance.

Expect the needs of the children and the home to consume all the time of an adult, especially in the first six months. In most countries, you'll need to expend a great deal of effort on the essentials of living. If both parents expect to share the ministry, then both must share the responsibility for the home and family.

If one of you has a specific assignment such as teaching, and the other bears most of the responsibility for logistics and parenting, anticipate that the "unemployed" one may have the hardest job and the most difficult time adjusting. The "employed" spouse has a ready-made structure, social context, and a support group of colleagues. The at-home spouse has to cope with the child's adjustments; repairs; procuring goods and services; and dealing with vendors, beggars, or others who come to the door. They may have an undefined role and no clear sense of purpose. Again, communicate. That may provide the key to making it in your radically different setting.

Reentry

The more deeply your family becomes involved in the host culture, and the more emotionally significant your experience, the more readjusting you'll have to do when you return. Children may find a shrunken circle of friends that doesn't appreciate new global perspectives. When reentering, put into use the same kinds of skills and activities that prepared your family for the separation, loss, and cultural change of going overseas.

You'll probably bring back more than you realize: a wealth of family experiences, new friendships, a broadened world view, and an appreciation and acceptance of difference.

Back in America, teachers often remarked on how creative my children were, a remark often made about missionary kids who grow up where amusements such as impromptu stories aren't a thing of the past. My eldest daughter, now an English literature major, carries those bedtime stories and Liberian friendships with her still.

23

Suddenly Significant Others

Romance on the field

by Teri Bulicek and Linda Olson

Teri Bulicek, Assistant Dean of the Chapel at Gordon College, and Linda Olson, National Director of STIM Resources for InterVarsity, have been involved in short terms as both singles and marrieds. They currently advise singles before, during, and after short terms.

Never before had Janice experienced such spiritual intimacy as she had with her teammate Tom. The beauty of Kenya along with the excitement of God's work in the Kenyan Church seemed to help kindle a special warmth between them. After a few late-night conversations, they began to realize that a special relationship was developing. They seemed so perfect together. But they had agreed to the mission board's policy that they would not use this short-term experience to pursue any kind of dating relationship. What should they do?

Tom and Janice's experience is not unusual. Short-term experiences seem to encourage intimate relationships. Among a team of short-term missionaries, friendships are often intensified by culture shock, by the narrowed field of relational options, by the long and erratic schedule, and by the bit of loneliness everyone feels. Infatuation can strike with other missionaries, and certainly with people of the host country.

Most mission agencies discourage dating relationships during a summer or year-long venture. Here's why:

- Romance ruins team life. The relationship is exclusive, leaving you cut off from the normal rhythm of team dynamics.
- A romantic relationship diverts you from the work. When you are distracted from what God has called you to do, the host church or team can't accomplish what it hoped to.
- You're the loser in terms of the personal growth you might have experienced during your short term.

- Special relationships often wreck the witness of the entire mission to the community, Christian or otherwise. Most short-termers would be horrified to discover what assumptions are made in most other cultures about "small" public displays of affections.

The short-term experience is just that—*short* and *intense*, lacking a broad "homeside" experience needed to develop and prove solid relationships. Although God could use a short-term experience to introduce you to a mate, in all likelihood it is the intensity of the experience which heightens the need for closeness and bonding.

Keep in mind these guidelines:

- Avoid exclusive relationships. Build relationships in the context of your entire team.
- Know the cultural rules in male/female relationships. Steer clear of every potentially questionable situation with the opposite sex, regardless of their nationality.
- Seek a leader's counsel *immediately* if something develops. Talk about things honestly and frankly.
- If, through others' counsel, God seems to be directing your lives together, resolve to wait until you have fulfilled your commitment overseas to pursue the relationship at home.

24

Prayer Power

Short-term prayer with long-term effect

by Robert Munger

Robert Munger is the chaplain to faculty and Pastor-at-Large at Fuller Theological Seminary.

As you go on your short term, prayer may be one of your biggest joys—and one of your biggest struggles. To help live your short term to the fullest, let's take a look at Jesus as He taught His followers to pray in the midst of ministry.

You already know that prayer is important. You can see it in Jesus' life. He prayed early; He prayed late; He prayed all night. He prayed alone; He prayed with others. He prayed with confidence; He prayed in deep agony. He even prayed on the cross. And He teaches us to pray.

The Purpose of Prayer

In our eagerness to get things done for the Lord, we often lose sight of the point of it all. God wants you to work for His glory, but He also wants you to "enjoy Him forever," as the Westminster Confession puts it. "Forever" includes the days of your short term. The first command is to love the Lord with all your heart, soul, mind, and strength. It doesn't say to work for Him with all you have, but to love Him with all you are. You can't love someone you don't know.

Don't allow the pressure of activities or the demands of duties on your short term crowd out time for personal communion with God. Take time to listen and talk with this Friend, and tell Him how you feel about yourself, about your relationship with Him, and about the world around you. Let Him tell you how He feels about you, what He has done for you, and what, with His help, you may do for Him.

Prayer is essential to do the work of God. In fact, prayer allows God to do His work through us. It's His way of receiving all the glory for what He accomplishes through our labor. As we see Him answer prayer, we see that He is indeed an active, living, and loving God. And so does the world.

To take time for prayer is never easy; at least it remains a constant struggle for me. But I've been learning how to follow Jesus' example in a few practical ways.

The Priority of Prayer

I give prayer priority, as Jesus did (Luke 6:12). You should schedule regular time with the Lord each day. It's often best at the start of the day when you're mentally alert. Put it down as an appointment in your date book, if you keep one. Consider it your most important appointment. Ask God to help you keep it and fill it with His presence.

Regular time is more productive than occasional longer periods of time, so plan for and anticipate it as you would a meeting with the most significant, dearly loved person you know. Don't consider it a duty or assignment to be done to fulfill requirements. Welcome it as an opportunity for sharing your heart with your most treasured companion.

When you schedule time, be sure that your goals aren't your lord. If you focus on the schedule instead of on your relationship with Jesus, you'll find yourself feeling guilty when you can't spend the time you'd expected. Don't wallow in guilt. Confess to the Lord if you're not spending the scheduled time with Him. (Be *sure* to acknowledge His forgiveness.) Then change your goals to make them more realistic, if necessary. Tell someone, too. Having someone encourage you can help keep the whole process in perspective.

Using captured time is one way to keep from being trapped in guilt over a grueling schedule. In the routine of things, brief moments occur when you can have quick conversation with the Lord, such as when waiting for a bus, walking to the market, or standing in line. Be ready for such opportunities. Situations will present themselves; moments will suddenly surface.

You don't have to pray a certain type of prayer. Maybe you only have time to make a comment like, "Wow, Jesus, send more laborers to reach this city," or "Lord, give me a person to share the Gospel with here," or "Lord, how do You feel about that lady and child I saw on the bus? Does Your heart ache like mine?" Impromptu conversations express close companionship with the Friend with whom we move through the hours.

Occasionally plan for extended time in prayer. Schedule a few hours during a special morning or evening, or take an entire day or weekend, if your time and co-workers permit. You can spend extended time in prayer alone or with others. As you do this, you'll again be following the example of Jesus; He spent extended time in prayer more than once.

Several hours will allow you to settle into prayer and praise and to dig deeply into what God is doing and can do on your short term. You may need to devote extended time for earnest intercession for the urgent spiritual and physical needs you've seen around you.

The Place of Prayer

Have a place for prayer. Jesus did (Luke 4:42; 22:39). Jesus' counsel is to go into your room and shut the door (Matt. 6:6). Meeting regularly with God in a particular place quickens faith by reminding us of past gracious encounters with Him, building faith in His presence and provision. Your place may be a quiet corner, an open field, an office before others arrive, or, if you'll be traveling a lot, wherever you lay your head. When you first arrive on your short term, ask God to help you find a place to meet with Him, and earnestly search for it.

The Power of Prayer

To be fresh in prayer, pray with an open Bible. Vital prayer is more than a monologue or recital of requests; it's a conversation in which two or more participate. Jesus teaches that we are to live "on every word that comes from the mouth of God" (Matt. 4:4). We're to listen for that word, hear it, and eagerly respond to it.

I find it helpful to let Him begin the conversation by listening to what He is saying to me through the Bible and allowing Him to give direction to my petitions. Look for promises in Scripture, and ask God to fulfill them. More importantly, search earnestly for His commands and concerns. When God's will is being done, His promises are being fulfilled.

Also, pray with a team, because there is power in united prayer. Christianity is personal, but never solitary. To function fully under His direction in the power of the Holy Spirit, knowing His mind and doing His will, we need one another (I Cor. 12:12-26).

Gather as few as two or three to form a prayer team. That seems to be the pattern Jesus indicated when He said, "if two of you on earth agree about anything you ask for, it will be done for you by my Father in heaven. For where two or three come together in my name, there am I with them" (Matt. 18:19-20). Observe the scope of the promise in this text. Observe the conditions: agree with Christ and one another in the unity of the Spirit. And observe the assurance: it will be done. Where two or more teammates are able to pray together with common convictions and concerns, there is spiritual impact.

These prayer times can become great times of relationship building. Honestly share positive and negative experiences and feelings. Support one another in caring love and build each other up in faith and obedience.

When you pray, whether alone or with a group, be sure to make your requests specific and expect specific answers. If you pray for Abdullah's salvation, pray for specific indications of his interest in the Gospel. If you're praying for your teammate Joe's needs, tell God what the answer to your prayer may look like. That way you can see the answers and be glad.

Finally, be thankful. Once again, Jesus is your example here. He was always thanking the Father. Continually thanking God will help you to live with the most Christ-like attitude, whether you're having trouble sleeping or loving a teammate. Thank God for His presence in every situation and condition, whether it be one of sickness or joy, failure or fruitfulness.

25

Bible Steady

Keeping in the Word while doing the work

by Virgil Amos

Virgil Amos is General Director of Ambassadors Fellowship, a mission organization with a special focus on involving minorities in missions around the world.

Most believers struggle to keep disciplined in Bible study during the most routine days in the predictable, settled environment of their home. Imagine how easy it is to abandon personal Bible study during busy short-term ministries in far-off places.

Think of all the adjustments to make. The clocks seem to run differently: they're either too fast and everyone seems overworked and out of time, or they're too slow and people just hang out. There isn't enough to do.

Your living situation is usually different from home. It can be noisy; crowded; and without electricity, safety, or even privacy. And there's a physical challenge. Food can be tough to cope with. Sleep can be hard to get. Low-grade fevers can hit at odd times. Exhaustion or emotional stress can knock out anyone.

It's sad to see some short-termers try to "glide" through all of this irregularity. Some figure they've reached sufficient spiritual altitude before the mission so they can coast overseas and not crash before they get home. But they can end up as spiritual kamikazes, nearly committing spiritual suicide trying to get work done for God. Don't try it.

Satan wants a strange sort of urgent complacency for you. It's something like sleepwalking. You're in motion, but useless. Don't find yourself swordless in the battle. Commit yourself to keep in God's Word during your short term.

Build Convictions by Seeking God

Be sure that you really desire a strong life in God's Word. If you're just telling yourself that you *should* do this or *ought* to do that, you'll fall into a trap of guilt.

How do you strengthen your convictions? Refresh yourself in

the truth of how inadequate you really are to serve God on your own. Grasp anew the truth of how much God longs to communicate with you. He has plans to transform you by His word. Realize how much you could miss and how truly useless you might be without daily exposure to the Word of God.

Above all, set your heart to seek God. Get hungry for God. If you keep working up an appetite for God Himself, then you'll find yourself drawn to His word.

Ask God to bring you to this place of conviction in His own way. Write down your request to God in a notebook, date it, and review it regularly so that you can readily cooperate with God as He answers your prayer.

Discipline Yourself by Anticipating Distractions

Discipline is the learned habit of submitting your daily living to the priorities God is giving you. Overseas, you are going to be surrounded by all kinds of good things to do. Don't fall into the trap of trying to do them all. Discipline only really starts when you get free from other good activities worthy of your time.

If you allow conflicts with individuals with whom you are working, mission policies, or other conditions to divert you from Bible study, you will be greatly hindered in your study. If your activities are governed largely by your feelings or moods, you will find added difficulty in being consistent in study.

Anticipate distractions. What has hindered you before? Determine that no "ifs" will keep you from the Word: "if the weather is right; if I don't feel too tired; if I get my letters written." Maintain a steady frame of mind in the midst of interruptions. James 1:2 tells us to count trials as all joy. This joyful attitude will help you have and maintain a good attitude when faced with unexpected change.

Keep Flexible by Making Plans

Make a plan for study. It doesn't have to be perfect. A poor plan can be improved; it is better than no plan. Planning ahead doesn't mean being rigid or unspiritual. Only when you have a plan are you free to change or adjust in response to new circumstances.

Try to plan your study in the first part of the day. If interruptions do come, you still have the rest of the day. If you are a night person, you might do your study after others have gone to bed, provided there is sufficient lighting and no "lights out" curfew.

Plans are only facilitators. Try not to waste emotional energy worrying or feeling frustrated when you can't execute your plans. Adjust to the situation and press forward in faith (Phil. 3:13,14).

Keep Focused by Varying Your Method

There is no best method for study. A method is good only if it enables you to draw out from the Word the message that the Author intended. In Bible study, the student wants to know:

- What does the Scripture say?
- What does the passage mean (in context)?
- How can I apply the message to my present situation?

A bookmark could make the difference for you. Keep reading through selected books. A bookmark shows you where you left off. Just open the book there at any time and keep reading. (Don't try to "study" if you are just reading.)

The hardest part of Bible study is to keep motivated. So try different approaches to keep your interest. Devise your own. Here are just a few to get you started:

- Start with concerns that arise during your short term. Find answers to questions that arise while you serve. Better yet, find biblical ways to ask the same questions.
- Read a passage over and over for an entire week. Memorize the key verse. Share it. Let it sink into your bones.
- Pray through passages. Say them back to God in your own words. Use them in group prayer. Write letters home sprinkled with the truths you're learning.
- Read Scripture out loud to yourself.
- If you are learning the local language, try to study a passage in a local translation by comparing it to a good English translation.

The key to any ongoing effort to study Scripture is to *do* what you *hear* (James 1:22). Your short term overseas could be the best chance you'll ever have to grow in your Bible study life. That's because you are already in daily, intensive action for God. With so many opportunities to obey God directly, you're bound to understand His word more and more. Don't miss out on such an opportunity to know God. Keep in the Word.

26

Writers Keepers

How to keep a journal during your short term

by Mark Labberton

Mark Labberton has kept a journal in India, Bangladesh, Zimbabwe, and now in London, England, where he is pursuing a Ph.D.

We may come back from our summer breathless, carrying trays full of slides. But will we also come back with changed lives? Without even realizing it, we can find ourselves feeding on experience (which demands only activity) and miss the nourishment of wisdom (which requires reflection). During a short-term mission, with its pace and intensity, this tendency becomes all the greater. But God wants us to grow in wisdom. The writer of Proverbs puts it plainly, "Wisdom is supreme; therefore get wisdom. Though it cost all you have, get understanding" (Prov. 4:7).

Why Keep a Journal

We "keep" journals but "write" letters. Think of your journal as a treasure where you store the experiences God is giving you. As you remember them, God can turn them into wisdom.

Realize that working for and with Christ in a new world that you don't understand can be a life-changing gift. If you just coast through the experience and move on, you may miss the growth God wants to give you as a disciple. Forgetfulness can be your excuse for immaturity. But remembrance, the Bible assures us, is essential to the way of wisdom.

Your cross-cultural experience is like being seated at a great feast. You can't take everything in at one sitting. You can listen, smell, touch, taste, and savor only a little bit of what lies before you at one time. It all begins the moment the first rush of humid air hits you in the face as you step off the plane in Manila, or in the first evening you smell the dung fires as they are lit for cooking in Calcutta, or in the early morning when you hear the sounds of unfamiliar birds on the Serengeti Plain, or in the call to prayer piercing the mid-afternoon heat in Istanbul.

At these moments, the feast is real and clear. Experience the tastes and smells, the thoughts and emotions, the insights and questions, the remembrances and dreams. But unless you capture and clarify them, these first sensations will leave quickly as other experiences tumble in upon them. A journal is the perfect place to record this feast. It allows you to consider and savor the experience in order to digest it and gain the nourishment of wisdom from it.

Writing in your journal is like chewing your food. Once the first course is digested, you'll be able to more deeply experience and enter into each course that follows. However, if you haven't digested your initial experience, you'll probably start getting full and won't have as much capacity to take in more.

Sometimes it's hard to sense what you're feeling, know what you're learning, or see where you're going unless you write it down. Sure, you might be able to talk things out with somebody else, but your conversation will soon evaporate. You may find it difficult to share at an early stage with your teammates, or find it inappropriate to express yourself to your hosts. If you write in a journal, you can speak in any degree of intensity, in any kind of order (or chaos), or in any style you choose.

Later in the feast, when you feel acquainted with what is before you, but frustrated with the people, the food, or the pace (or lack of it), a journal can be a place to think, feel, and pray. A journal makes a difference months into your short term.

When you return home, your particular opportunity for cross-cultural experience will have passed. Immediately, the lightning speed of your life will resume. You come back to school, to a job, or to move and start other new responsibilities in ministry. In a few short months, your summer mission seems like ancient history.

You know you're to be a responsible steward of the opportunity God has given, but with the passing of time and the activity of the moment, the memories of the summer can easily begin to blur. Perhaps you forget the rough parts, or you only remember those parts and forget the easier and more enjoyable ones. You may find yourself reducing your experience to the three- or four-sentence reply you give when a casual friend asks, "So, how was it in Mombozombo?" Your journal will enable you to continue feeding on what has happened as you reread portions of it and as you continue to write.

Your journal will also enable you to be a better communicator of your experience by helping you to share precisely some of the anecdotes and a bit of your feelings. It can be a great tool to help you remember what you saw, how you felt, and what you learned. It will help you to communicate vivid stories that breathe life into your times of sharing with large groups such as your church or campus fellowship.

How to Keep a Journal

The first thing in keeping a journal is to decide to do it. If you don't already keep a journal, do you want to? If so, why? Are you willing to try keeping a journal as an experiment? If you do keep a journal, are you going to continue it over your short term? All the suggestions in the world about how to write an effective short-term journal will do no good unless your answers to these questions satisfy you. Once you've chosen to write a journal, you'll be able to keep at it.

To write a useful journal:

1. Write for yourself. A journal is private. You don't have to write it in a closet and place it under lock and key, but it's wise to keep it out of sight of those who may be tempted to read it, or whose culture doesn't forbid their reading it. It's private because your motive in writing is for personal exploration and growth, not for a grade or for publication.

Don't be paralyzed by trying to write your autobiography. Chances are, your "memoirs" will never be published. Relax. You're the only audience. As in all things, God will be your companion and teacher, but the workbook you develop before Him is whatever you make it.

2. Be yourself in *what* you write. God sees and knows everything. He knows how you're feeling and what you're thinking and doing. And He loves you. During your summer of ministry, you will be trying in every way possible to express that God knows people fully and still loves them where they are. In keeping a journal, you have a good opportunity to practice what you preach. Dare to trust that you can't surprise God by what you write. Honesty about the full range of your thoughts and emotions will not cause Jesus to love you any less, and may allow you to love Him and recognize His love for you all the more.

3. Be yourself in *how* you write. Some people keep a journal like a logbook. They find that lists of experiences, details, and prayer requests are most helpful as they think about what they're going through. Others use a stream-of-consciousness style, which may include lists, sentences, poems, illustrations, glue-in memorabilia, and whatever else they find inspiring. Still others write in letter form to God or to themselves. Many find a narrative style to be most natural to them, and they fill their journal with the behind-the-scenes details of what's really happening.

Your journal doesn't have to be like Jim Elliot's or Amy Carmichael's. And it *shouldn't* be. After all, you're not either one of them, and you never will be. You're uniquely created for a unique purpose. Your journal doesn't have to be great prose or full of lilting poetry. (You're not Hemingway or Shakespeare, either.) Trying to write like someone else will only cramp your style.

Whatever style you choose, and whether you use an empty book or a loose-leaf binder, a small, plain book with no lines or a flowered one with wide lines, do it your way and revel in its being your own. It may be the only thing all summer that is.

4. Be consistent but flexible about *when* you write. You don't have to write in your journal every fifth hour or even every fifth day. Some people view journal-keeping like other disciplines. As such, they find it helpful to do it regularly and at the same time; for example, each evening before bed or just after dinner. Often the style of summer missions is such that you won't have the sort of consistent schedule that makes this type of pattern easy. If you want to use your journal as a personal discipline, it can be a great tool. But in order to keep it up, you may want to seek the support and help of your teammates in arranging the schedule and place where you can spend 15 to 30 minutes each day writing.

If you approach journal-keeping with a definite structure in mind, please remember: as a discipline, it's meant to be a means of grace, not guilt. If you don't write in your journal for a week or two—or even a month—don't let it get you down.

I usually think of journal-keeping as a gift. I don't have to, but I get to. It's not the only way to get the most from my experience, and it certainly isn't worth feeling guilty if I don't. But it is a delightful and deeply enriching part of a short-term experience. I write in my journal as frequently as I can or want to, often in the short transitions between places or activities. At other times, I find I like writing for an hour or longer at the end of a week. And there are times when I don't feel like writing, but I do anyway. I'm always glad that I did.

When All is Said and Done

However and whenever you write in or read your journal, enjoy the fact that God is always there as a listener and comforter, guide and teacher. It's out of the real stuff of our lives and experiences that the fire of His love will purify and mold us. This is the way we will grow in wisdom. But let me warn you. In the midst of it all, don't let your journal become a way to hide from teammates or others to whom God has called you to minister. And don't allow your reflections to become more important than the real people and experiences with which God will surround you. That will defeat your journal's very purpose. Allow it to be the means by which you slow down and chew rather than ravenously consume your short-term experience.

As one person has observed, "To say that going to church will make us a Christian is like saying that going into the garage will make us a car." So it is with journal-keeping. In itself, it won't make us become wise any more than going on a short-term ministry project will automatically make us obedient and thoughtful World Christians. Ultimately, wisdom and obedience are functions of grace and of decisions.

The Kingdom of God needs people of wisdom, not just experience. May you return with slides that help you celebrate all the remarkable moments God provides in your short-term experience. May you also return with a journal under your arm and with a mind and heart full of newfound wisdom.

Some Practical Tips Before You Go

- Don't assume that traveler's checks are easily exchanged. Small denominations can be nice, but in some places, every check is taxed. Personal checks will probably not be received except by co-workers in your mission. A few credit cards are received overseas. If you take them, guard them well.

- Write down your passport number, expiration date, and place issued. Photocopying your passport is illegal. A copy of your birth certificate or marriage license can be helpful.

- Take pictures of your family to show your new friends. Most cultures greatly value family ties. Examine photos carefully. Leave behind any that display your family as frivolously wealthy or in what could be considered indecent attire.

- Arrange all needed visas carefully according to the guidance of your mission agency.

- Pack *lightly*. Walk around the block carrying everything you'll be taking with you; then decide if you can do with a little less.

- Pack and dress appropriately and inconspicuously. Leave behind outrageous fashions. Bring at least one dressy outfit and at least one fairly casual outfit. Check with your mission about climate and dress. You might plan to buy some of your clothing in the country.

- Check ahead for appropriate gifts from your home country to bring to your hosts.

- Bring addresses of people (especially supporters) at home.

- Because the voltage and amperage of electricity may be different, consider doing without electrical appliances. If you do need them, it could be wise to bring correct transformers and adapters to power your gadgets.

- Explain to your close friends who are expecting regular correspondence that the postal service can be erratic. You may want to plan a numbering system for your correspondence so it will be evident if one of the letters is lost.

- Empty your wallet or purse of documents that you won't need, such as a fishing license or library card.

27

Great Expectations

How to handle the certain surprise of reality

by Bob Howell

Bob Howell is vice-president of Administrative Services at CRISTA Ministries, and formerly was director of Personnel for LIFE Ministries.

What do you expect from your short-term experience? Knowing your expectations is one of the most important ways you can prepare for your time overseas.

Maybe you don't think you have any expectations. If so, you're in for a shock, because a hidden expectation which clashes with reality is always surprising. Expectations come from parents, teachers, friends, literature, and a whole range of other sources, but mostly they come from you.

Preparing for a short term is a bit like smelling baking bread when you're hungry. The anticipation of it makes your mouth water. People have given money to help you. They're praying for you. You're on a mission, so you expect that certain things are going to happen.

I know what it's like when people in my mission arrive for their summer in Japan. They've been commissioned by their church. Often they think that they're going to lead many into the Kingdom of God. They're going to do this by being friendly and outgoing. They are, in fact, going to turn Japan around because of their experience.

But when they get to Japan, they go through training which isn't the glorious experience they'd thought and talked about. It's hot. It's muggy. There are crowds of people everywhere. They haven't been able to witness on the street yet. When they finally get a chance, no one understands them.

Finally, the training ends. They are introduced to their church, which they find has only 15-20 members. The English classes, in which they'd hoped to meet a lot of Japanese, have four or five students signed up for the whole summer.

At this point, their expectations could be dashed, especially if they don't like the food, they're not used to a hot, humid climate, and they don't enjoy the crowded oriental suburbs. They might form new expectations—very dismal ones, at best.

The best way to avoid this kind of disappointment is to evaluate your expectations before you go. Are they realistic? Have you based them on the right motives?

There's nothing wrong with high expectations. William Carey said, "Attempt great things for God, and expect great things from God." That kind of thinking gives you high motivation. I'm not suggesting that you lower your hopes or lessen your vision for God's glory. I would, however, like to suggest that you add a few expectations, if you haven't done so already.

Frustration. Expect to be frustrated. No matter what your situation, you'll always be encountering the unexpected. God will often use the difficult and the unforeseen to do great things in your life and in the lives of others. If you don't have some frustration, you probably aren't learning and growing.

Forgiveness. Expect to forgive. You will make mistakes; you'll need to forgive yourself and ask for forgiveness from others. Others will make mistakes; they won't understand you, and they'll hurt you. If you expect this, you'll be ready to learn many lessons that God wants to teach you. You'll learn a lot about acceptance: how to accept those who don't agree with you, and how to accept yourself when you don't perform the way you think you should.

Flexibility. Expect to be flexible. You might be tired of hearing about flexibility, but that continues to be one of the most valuable words to remember as you go overseas. Adapt. Fit into the situation. Allow God to use you any way He wants. Yield yourself to Him. Tell Him, "I want to obey You, whatever the situation."

If your desire is simply to glorify God, you can look at situations in a refreshing way. You can realize that God is honored no matter how much or how little you are able to do. Constantly looking for an opportunity to share Jesus Christ will keep your motivation high, your flexibility strong, your frustration low, and your expectations in perspective.

Our God, after all, is the same one Paul was talking about when he said, "...him who is able to do immeasurably more than all we ask or imagine..." (Eph. 3:20). God will use you and bless you beyond your expectations. That's one expectation you can count on being met.

28

Culture Clash

How to ease the shock

by Laurel A. Cocks

Laurel A. Cocks enjoys preparing people for cross-cultural service in her role as coordinator of Pre-Field Orientation at Missionary Internship.

"Our new short-termers have launched guerrilla warfare against anything with wings or six legs. They set timetables and expect to keep them."

Reading Joy's letter, I couldn't help but laugh as I pictured a couple of Americans in battle fatigues launching an attack on gigantic insects, and then, flushed and panting, trying vainly to accomplish everything else on their list. But my laughter died as I read further the closely typed pages. Joy was reacting indignantly toward these people, and I needed to know why.

The short-termers had come to a beautiful African country for three months to help out with a specific project. But two weeks after their arrival, nothing seemed very exotic or spiritual. In fact, it wasn't just the insects they were attacking, but also the local food, the clothes, the health habits, the driving rules (or lack of them), and the multitude of other things that were culturally uncomfortable for them.

Perhaps such reactions and behavior are to be expected when people arrive in a foreign country. After all, there's a lot of newness to handle. Aren't they entitled to a little grumbling in exchange for the great sacrifice they're making to come to this place where everything is so strange?

My friend Joy doesn't think so, and neither do the nationals who are watching them. As she thinks about them, Joy feels a mixture of emotions—sadness, frustration, shame, helplessness. She doesn't know where she should begin to counter their attitudes, or if anything she says will help at all.

Though Joy is also a short-termer, she doesn't seem to have gone through much of what we've come to call culture shock. She likes her new country and finds it fascinating to learn what makes people tick. She wouldn't say it has all been easy or that there are no problems or strains, but she feels content.

What makes the difference? Her personality? Her preparation? Are some people destined to adjust to another culture with minimal discomfort, while others battle it continually and then come home hurt and soured?

Losses and Gains

Let's see what happens when a person moves into another culture. In some ways, it's not so different from any change we make in life. Remember when you were a child and your family moved to a new town; when you went from junior high to high school; when you started a new job? The new experiences piled up until you were on overload. And your inner computer was saying, "Can't continue." You may have cried, binged on pizza, locked yourself in your room, gone for long runs, or done whatever you do to deal with stress. It seemed the disorientation would never end, but somehow it did, and you made it.

You were being hit by a series of losses and gains, and it wasn't easy to manage them. When you go into another culture, you experience similar kinds of losses and gains, but in a more intense way. It's helpful to identify some of them so that when you begin your short-term assignment, you'll recognize them.

Losses you may experience:
- Support from family and friends from church or school.
- Familiar ways of communicating and relating to people, nonverbally as well as verbally.
- Knowing how to act and what's expected of you.
- A familiar setting that provides security and a sense of worth.

Things you stand to gain:
- A new setting and all the sights, tastes, smells, and sounds that go with it.
- New acquaintances who will be new friends and co-workers.
- New language, patterns of speech, and nonverbal cues.
- A new role, identity, or position within a different society.

There's usually a short honeymoon period when you first enter a new culture. You've looked forward to this time with great anticipation, and it's really exciting to be there at last. However, some find the first few days and weeks to be the hardest. As in everything else, we're all created differently. About a third of the way through a short term, most people take a nose dive out of the honeymoon and into reality. This may be especially true when they're mostly with the local population rather than with Americans. Severe climatic (and climactic) changes and illness also play a part.

The gains mentioned above may begin to seem more like insurmountable barriers than things to be treasured. The streets seem dirty and noisy. The market, which looked colorful and exciting in the travel guide, smells strange and is filled with foods that are anything but tempting. And you can't just look. You have to purchase food items in odd amounts, using different currency and a new language.

A national you're longing to get to know arrives an hour late, and his only excuse is that he stopped to talk with a friend. People smile at your attempts to speak their language, and then prefer to use their limited English instead of helping you. At a military checkpoint, soldiers ask to look in your boot and laugh uproariously when you show them your sandal. You're doing go-for jobs for a missionary who doesn't always seem to understand that he has to take time from his busy schedule to plan your time. How can anyone in his or her right mind call these gains?

What's happening during this time is the meeting and clashing of differences. It inevitably causes uneasiness. Before you know it, you feel frustrated, embarrassed, tense, and confused. You may be tired and want to sleep all the time, or you may have trouble sleeping. You may be irritable, even a bit depressed and homesick, with diarrhea and a headache thrown in, too.

There can be some enjoyable and highly amusing incidents during this time, if only you have eyes to see. Take that experience with the boot at the military checkpoint. To make soldiers laugh because you don't know the trunk of your car from your shoe is certainly a lot better than having them angry with you—and it makes a great story to tell when you get home. It's not always easy to laugh at yourself, but that's a quality to work on during your short term. It's simply a fact of life that misunderstanding and disharmony will result when differences meet. Just remember that this doesn't necessarily mean that you're less spiritual or less loved by God. Then let yourself laugh.

It's crucial to realize that you can choose how you'll react to cultural differences. You can decide to approach a situation or person within a new culture with acceptance, openness, and trust. If you begin this way, you're more likely to work through the frustrating, difficult times and arrive at understanding and mutual respect.

You may be wondering, "Isn't it risky to be open? Won't you get hurt and regret it if you accept someone too quickly?" It's true that there are risks involved in this, as in any human relationship. But consider the alternative: if you approach the other culture with suspicion, fear, and prejudice, you face the risk of alienation and isolation from the very people you came to get to know and serve. The choice is yours.

Dealing With Culture Stress

Here are some practical ideas that many short-termers have found helpful when feeling the stress of a new culture.

1. Talk it out:

- Talk with a national friend. Lois prayed for such a friend before she and her husband left Canada. Her new friend helped her understand many of her new experiences, introduced her to relatives and friends, and was a great help in preventing loneliness. (Single people aren't the only ones who get lonely, you know.)

- Talk with your spouse or housemate. It's helpful to describe your feelings to others. This may prevent the explosion that sometimes occurs when emotions remain bottled up. It's also a good idea to get another person's perspective so that your few bad experiences don't outweigh all the good ones. One caution here: there are some things that should be told to God alone. Simply dumping everything on another person may do neither of you any good.

- Talk with other expatriates. It may be interesting to share your experiences with fellow short-termers, missionaries, or others who have lived for some time in the country. The latter may have forgotten what it was like when they first arrived, so don't be too disappointed if they find it hard to empathize. Try to avoid, though, spending time with any foreigner who looks down on the nationals and their culture. Some people delight in telling disparaging stories about the "natives." The disease can be contagious, so don't expose yourself to it.

- Talk to yourself by journaling and letter writing. Writing can be very therapeutic, so articulate your thoughts and feelings on paper. Journals don't talk back, and you don't have to regret what you say to them. A young woman who spent a year with an African family enjoyed writing out her prayers and meditations. These were later an encouragement to those with whom she shared them. Your letters to close friends and relatives back home give them insights into your life abroad and keep home ties intact. If you find writing difficult, why not talk into a tape recorder?

2. Get into a routine. Language study provides routine for some people. It brings order to the day and gives built-in opportunities to get to know people and learn the culture. If no structure is provided, build a certain amount of it for yourself, remembering to leave room for God to bring unexpected people and experiences into your life.

If your job involves moving from place to place, try to schedule sufficient time to rest and get used to the new place. Don't feel you have to play the tourist and try to see every sight within a 200-mile radius.

3. Try to learn the local language. Learning a person's language is an indication of your respect and acceptance. You may not get too far beyond greetings if your term is short, but you're sure to be rewarded with smiles and good will. Even if they know English, most people appreciate your effort. Language learning also helps form deeper relationships. And more than that, it's a way to minister to people.

4. Learn all you can. Observe, listen, inquire. Try to make sense out of the information you gather by making some tentative guesses. Then check them out with someone. Never be afraid to admit your first hunch was wrong. Throw it out and try again. Making a game of it can be fun and informative, and you'll be surprised how much it helps the blues.

When I was first in Zambia, another greenhorn and I were wondering about a strange object just outside the church door. It was a small bunch of dry grass tied together at one end. My friend, who had been reading all about religious customs, thought it must have had something to do with spirit worship; a strange thing to have near a church. When we asked, we discovered it was just a broom used to sweep the building. So much for that guess. I'm glad we hadn't drawn any firm conclusions from our first observations.

Develop an inquisitive mind for history, social customs, religion, family structure, recreation, political organization, and anything

else you're interested in. Prepare your own list to take advantage
of the ideas in Robert Kohls' book, *Survival Kit for Overseas Living*
(Intercultural Press, 1984), or *Transcultural Study Guide* (Volunteers
in Asia, 1975) by Grey, Darrow, Morrow, and Palmquist.

Learn from everyone and everything you can. This will involve
learning the "rules" so you can inquire in a courteous way. Don't
let your curiosity come across as blunt, too interrogative, or impo-
lite. Instead, learn from situations and people so that you can return
to them as a friend. You can learn from nationals, anthropologists,
missionaries, and even those with whom you disagree. Accept their
point of view for what it is: information given from another perspective or world view.

5. Examine your expectations. You have them, whether or not
you think you do. Expectations usually hide in dark corners, not
articulated, and it takes some effort to flush them out. "What did I
expect?" is a question to keep asking yourself in order to get more
clarity between what you thought and what you got. Not dealing
with unmet expectations is a sure way to grease the slide of disappointment and disillusionment.

It's unlikely that you'll meet all your expectations. One short-
termer in the Philippines thought he'd be able to speak the language much sooner than he could. Another common expectation
is that a "successful" ministry is possible the minute you step off
the plane. Remember that success is not your primary goal. Instead,
look for ways to link up with what God is doing there. He'll use
you all right, but perhaps not as you expected. Positive, realistic
expectations are a most effective antidote for cultural stress. Don't
leave home without them.

6. Keep learning about your own culture. Don't wait until you
get overseas to start to understand your own cultural values and
perspectives. Karen was eager to teach English in China, but the
Lord knew what she needed first. At graduate school, she began to
see herself, a middle-class American, through the eyes of international students and professors. Values and attitudes she had previously taken for granted came up for examination. This deeper
understanding of her own culture and what lies behind her behavior is now enabling Karen to better learn the Chinese culture.

7. Use the opportunity to grow spiritually. Trust the Lord to use
the challenges and difficulties you face to develop stability in you.
When Sheila left the United States to do community development
work, she couldn't imagine herself as a missionary, and it worried

her. Would she be able to fulfill the role? Now after almost a year, she writes, "It's helped me to hear the firm beliefs of my staff as I flounder in the uneasiness of being foreign and alone. My time here has been a real growth experience in solitude." It has been important for Sheila to be a part of ongoing ministry, to see herself in God's scheme of things.

Much of your learning will occur weeks and months after you return home. As you recover from the rough spots, remember that they have the capacity to bring about deep changes in your life. You may then say, "Thank You, Lord, for the time overseas. I pray You'll one day lead me back."

29

Preparation

It takes more than packing your toothbrush

by Ray Howard

Ray Howard, Mountain/Central Regional Director for ACMC (formerly the Association of Church Missions Committees), helps churches in the Mountain and South Central states build strong missions programs. He and his wife Diana began their short-term service in Uruguay.

So you want to go on a short-term assignment. How do you get ready? Are there things you can begin doing now to help you be effective in learning and ministering in another culture while getting the most out of the experience? Yes! But you won't find them all in books and special training courses.

Since your cross-cultural experience doesn't take place primarily in a library or a classroom, your preparation shouldn't take place primarily in a school setting, either.

There are four key areas of your life to prepare: your heart, your hands, your head, and your feet. Almost every breakdown on the field (and there have been plenty of them) can be traced back to neglecting one of these four areas. Here are a few suggestions for how to prepare.

Preparation of the Heart

The Scriptures are filled with allusions to battle, warfare, and conflict. Although such spiritual conflict is subtly disguised within North America, it's much more tangible and overt in most other areas of the world. If you aren't equipped to handle it, you're in for real trouble.

There's no substitute for regular time alone with God to equip you for spiritual warfare through comfort, encouragement, and instruction. If you need help, ask for it. Seek help first from Him, and then from someone you know whose walk with God is obvious in his or her lifestyle. Ask that person to teach you and to hold you accountable in the areas of Bible study, meditation on the Scriptures, prayer, and Scripture memorization. Many resources are available to help you, so make use of them.

Consider setting aside a whole day or more as a preparatory spiritual retreat. Review Scriptures that encourage you and build up your faith. List and pray through all your concerns. Use a journal and ask the Holy Spirit to guide you in writing down measurable, realistic spiritual goals for your trip.

Preparation of the Hands

A great golf shot is composed of many individual components: a balanced stance, a good backswing, a solid downstroke, a smooth follow-through, and a steady eye on the ball. It takes practice to put it all together.

Any short-term assignment is composed of many specific activities, and most components can be developed before heading out. Be creative in finding ways to sharpen specific skills before you go.

If you know where you might be going, try to find someone from that country who can help you understand the customs of his or her homeland. This may also give a chance for you to share your faith across the same cultural barriers that you will face on your short term.

If there are students from that country on a nearby campus, try to build friendships. Learn how they interact and relate. Are they quiet or noisy, physically affectionate or reserved? When they talk, do they stand close together or far apart? Do they make eye contact? How appropriate is it for women to talk to men, and vice versa?

Any community of more than 100,000 people has a variety of cultures. Seeking them out and getting to know others different from yourself is an easy, but critically important, way to prepare. You might go to a nearby college and offer to tutor internationals in English. Or go to an ethnic neighborhood and talk to shopkeepers. Or find a predominantly ethnic church you can visit.

If you're going to be on a construction team, learn the names of tools in the language you will be using. Look for a friendly contractor who'll let you help out on his construction site for a few days. If you're going to be working with children, volunteer to help in your church's children's ministry. If you're going to be doing door-to-door evangelism, look for opportunities to do that, preferably in another cultural setting.

If you play an instrument or sing, and foresee the possibility of using those talents, prepare a few songs and bring the music with you. You may have the opportunity to give your testimony or speak. Prepare for this by writing out your testimony. (Stay within five minutes by keeping to the "I once was blind, but now I see" outline.) Jot down thoughts and Scripture references that you could use to give a short devotional message.

All these ideas will help you to feel a bit more ready, but many short-termers miss the obvious: get involved in ministry now. You already know that getting on a plane won't make you a valiant missionary. "As now, so then" has been a good rule of thumb for aspiring missionaries. Get involved *now* in the ministry or outreach of your local church. When you get to an overseas assignment, *then* you'll find yourself responding to ministry needs out of a backlog of experience.

Preparation of the Head

Moving into another culture is in many ways like becoming a four-year-old again. You don't know all that people are saying. You don't understand what it all means. Just as all human beings are different, so are all cultures. God's creativity is expressed as uniquely in cultures as it is in individuals. There are a number of books that can help you in the area of understanding culture and cultural change, but there are also some things you can do to get ready.

In addition to speaking with other North Americans freshly back from cross-cultural experiences, you can ask your international friends to share some of their first impressions of North America. That way you can begin to see your culture through the eyes of someone from another culture. If they're free to share deeply and honestly, and if you can hear them without getting defensive, their new insights will be tremendously valuable as you try to approach their culture with similar openness.

There are a number of simulation games and training tools that can be of real help in a group setting. One of these is the Luna Game (A.D. 2000 Global Services Office, Attn. Olgy Gary, 1869 Galbreth Rd. # 3, Pasadena, CA 91104).

A major hurdle that must be overcome when learning a new culture is the fear of feeling foolish and childish. You must remember that culturally you're on the level of a three- or four-year-old, and thus these feelings are both appropriate and acceptable. Try new things here at home, such as eating a whole meal in a Chinese restaurant with chopsticks (if this is new for you) or having a meal in a Middle Eastern or North African restaurant where you're required to eat with your fingers. Perhaps a friend or a missionary from your host country would be willing to prepare a meal that's typical of the area. The idea is not to be shocked but rather to be better prepared.

There may be some experiences for which there is no adequate preparation, like being expected, as the honored guest, to eat the chicken head floating in the soup, or sitting through the three-hour evening services (every night) in an unintelligible language at the end of hot days of construction when you're dog-tired (and a little sick) because you're being housed in the church, and a bench in the sanctuary is your bed.

But before all these fun experiences can happen, you have to get there, and this can be perhaps the most rewarding and faith-stretching aspect of the whole experience.

Preparation of the Feet

In II Corinthians 8 and 9, the apostle Paul saw the sharing of financial resources as a tremendously positive thing. Not only did it meet needs, but it also taught generosity and responsibility, gave people an opportunity to see God at work, and allowed God to bless people for their faithfulness.

Pray, look for, recruit, and train others to join you in this exciting, risky adventure. Give them "a piece of the action" and rejoice in God's work in their lives. Allow them to give you counsel and encouragement in raising the prayer and financial support necessary to make this short term a life-changing experience for everyone involved.

As you allow others to take part in your adventure, it will change not only your life, but also the lives of those with whom you share it. Make them a part of your preparation, your going, your returning, and your follow-through plans.

You say that asking people for money is a terribly humbling experience. You're right. But our example in this is Jesus, who gave up so much for us. Where in the Scriptures do you ever see personal pride portrayed as a positive thing? Carefully study II Corinthians 8 and 9, writing out in your own words the principles they contain. Then apply them in your own support raising.

Going overseas without preparation is like learning to swim by jumping out of a speeding boat. It's not a good idea. Your careful preparation will multiply the value of your cross-cultural service.

30
Entering "Closed" Countries
Tips for short-termers in tough situations

by Steve Chism

Steve Chism has led several short-term teams to under-evangelized people in cities in Asia and the Middle East.

Some experts estimate that more than 60 percent of the world is closed to traditional missionaries. Perhaps *closed* is the wrong word. *Closed* implies that Christians are locked out with no way to get in a country to do Christ's work.

In fact, Christian workers are serving in these countries, many on a short-term basis. If you are privileged to join missionaries in such a restricted-access country, you need to know how to help, and not inadvertently ruin, the efforts of Christian workers there.

Before you go, find out as much as you can about restrictions in the country to which you are going. Every situation is unique and changing. Never assume that the place you're going is free of restrictions. Generally, there will be slightly different sets of restrictions for missionaries and national Christians. Get acquainted with both.

Restrictions on Missionaries

Some countries, such as Saudi Arabia and Myanmar (formerly Burma), allow no open witness or service of any kind. Even so, some missionaries choose to witness and serve quietly in these countries without official permission. They usually try to carry on their work without ever being openly known as missionaries. In other countries, such as Ethiopia, India, and Thailand, missionaries often strive to work carefully within these regulations. Some choose to strategically push beyond the limits.

How to Work With Missionaries

• Don't assume missionaries want to be known by you. For them to keep a low profile means they sometimes keep a strategic distance from people who are co-laborers (such as you). If you do meet, it's often poor manners to ask about specifics of what they're doing. Let them choose what to tell you. Watch for signals that they would rather not say more.

- Expunge the word *missionary* from your vocabulary—even while you're talking with them. Use some terms very carefully. Red-flag words to avoid include *convert, evangelism, mission, crusade, the Gospel,* and many more.

- Trust the advice given you by your host missionaries. You may get conflicting counsel at times. That's often because the situation changes. Sometimes Christians disagree as to the most biblical and effective way to go. If you know that you're not going to follow instructions, most missionaries would greatly appreciate your distancing yourself from them, their converts, and their contacts.

Restriction on National Christians

Some national Christian groups are centuries-old minorities, known to be Christians by all. These Christians are usually allowed few freedoms to worship. They persist in gathering, despite stringent regulations and occasional surveillance.

In other countries, Christian gatherings may be officially disallowed or even fiercely opposed. Fellowships often continue secretly as house churches.

The Christians most vulnerable to official hostility and social pressure are new believers from dominant religions or in countries where it's actually considered a jail-worthy crime to convert to Christianity. A new believer may be a convert from a high Hindu caste or the son of a Muslim official. Each has unique pressures almost impossible for most short-termers to understand. Try anyway. They can ill afford to be brought into needless and dangerous confrontation with the dominant society because of your foolish mistakes.

Working With National Christians

- Don't assume that you're welcome to join in their gatherings. The nationals may feel obligated to invite you, even though they must endure the sometimes severe consequences of a conspicuous foreigner.

- Don't judge or be too eager to change things. Some of the practices may bother you. For example, Muslim converts may want to be baptized in secret. Or a church meeting may be billed as a birthday party. Most short-termers don't bring with them the needed experience to offer suggestions or changes to the situation. Your best option is to determine to serve and to follow instructions.

- Be careful about bringing Bibles and literature. They may be needed but may present an embarrassing situation if imported in an ill-advised way. Get counsel before you act as a self-appointed courier.

Before You Go

- Keep quiet. Use educated caution in announcing your trip to your church and community. Non-Christian visitors to your church can do serious damage. Home town newspapers sometimes can say too much. Explain the situation to your church leaders. Many short-termers are advised to be non-specific about their destination. Instead of saying Algeria, why not simply say you're headed for North Africa? If the Lord guides you to return to the country in the future for a longer term, you'll be glad that you worked to keep a low profile.

- Advise supporters and family. Help them understand that mail is often opened and read by authorities hostile to the Gospel. Make sure everyone grasps the serious ramifications of letters which mention missions or evangelism. Some people may not understand unless you specify which words or themes to omit from their letters. Help them understand why your letters must not tell of your evangelism.

- Pack carefully. Books and diaries which make your missionary purpose explicit may need to be left at home.

While in the Country

- Learn your identity so well that you can easily and honestly explain to anyone who you are and what you are doing. Be faithful to your identity. If you're a teacher, be a good one. If you're a student, study hard. If you're a tourist, then certainly do "touristy" things.

- Secret police are sometimes planted, pretending to be very eager seekers of truth. Work with your leadership in determining the motives of would-be converts. Be sure that you have the authority to welcome them to meetings or give them names and addresses of believers.

- Ask God for wisdom continually. Christ wants us to act with the wisdom of serpents while serving with the innocence of doves. Get wisdom from God. Keep close to Him. There's no other way to strike the balance of serpent and dove, make the hard decisions, do the work of God, and be at peace.

- Relax. Don't terrify yourself into some frenzy of covert activity. Be yourself. The whole point is to take care of basic security so you can carry on with the work. The situation is in God's hands. Give and serve and speak the Gospel. No true ministry worth doing is risk-free anyway. If you have taken basic precautions, you can leave the results to God.

31
Keeping Healthy
You can survive your short term

by Lynn Samaan

Lynn Samaan, Director of Spiritual Formation and Outreach at the Silverlake Presbyterian Church, has overseas experience in Africa, the Middle East, and Asia.

You may have nightmares of wasting away in the feverish delirium of some unknown tropical scourge. Relax. Most short-termers don't get seriously ill. But a few do, so keep in mind some practical things to help you prevent the worst and endure the most common maladies.

Before You Go

Pack a copy of your medical history, including your blood type, allergies, and any special conditions. If you wear glasses, bring a copy of your lens prescription. Contact lens wearers should check to see if it will be practical to wear and clean their lenses at their short-term location.

Check with your mission about any vaccinations you'll need. You may call your local Health Department for information about specific shots and where to get them. Your doctor can advise you regarding the vaccinations and any side effects. Be sure to keep your vaccinations current when traveling.

The mission agency should also tell you if you need to take a drug which helps to prevent malaria. The most common is chloroquine, for which you'll need a prescription. You need to begin taking this medication before you leave home, so be sure to look into it early.

Health insurance is a good idea. Review your policy and be familiar with the one your mission will have arranged for you.

While Overseas

"Don't drink the water!" That's probably the most common piece of health advice the traveler gets. Keeping healthy involves more than just watching your water supply. But it's really not all that complicated.

Get informed quickly about the particular health hazards in your locale. Every situation has its own set of parasites, insect-borne diseases, and foods to avoid. Make it your responsibility to get acquainted with potential problems that may vary from city to countryside or from season to season. If you know what you're up against, you can relax. It's common sense from there.

The first few days you're there, you may feel a bit ill. Most likely, it's only jet lag. The best way to treat jet lag is to adjust to your hosts' schedule as soon as possible. That means going to bed when they do and getting up when they do, even if you don't feel like it. Sometimes a short nap in the afternoon helps. But don't stretch it out. The sooner you get over your jet lag, the more fully you'll be able to enter into the ministry.

Practice whatever protection and prevention you can. Learn to use mosquito netting. Find where you can get purified water so you don't rot your teeth drinking bottled sodas.

In general, "drink it boiled and eat it hot." What about questionable food and drinks offered to you? It can be a tough choice. If you seal yourself off in antiseptic isolation from the people, you might as well have stayed at home. But if you lay waste to your body by not being careful about what you ingest, you could be in bed the entire time you're overseas. That's of little value. Follow the counsel of your mission leaders.

What if you *do* get sick? Don't panic. You probably won't die, though you may feel like you want to. Most overseas maladies have been faced before. Here are some common ones.

Diarrhea can strike for a variety of reasons: food poisoning, viral infection, amebic dysentery, or other causes. You won't know right away what's causing it, and usually no medication is needed.

If diarrhea strikes, be sure to drink plenty of liquids to keep from becoming dehydrated. It's good to drink water with a bit of sugar and salt (and some orange juice, if you have it). Good foods to eat include bananas, chicken, potatoes, and hot cereal. Avoid raw fruits and greasy or highly seasoned foods. If your condition persists for more than four days without improvement, or if other complications follow, you should see a doctor.

Vomiting can hit for all the same reasons as diarrhea, and a few more. Keep calm and keep yourself hydrated by sipping some clear drink. If vomiting goes on for more than a day, or if there are complications, see a doctor.

Short blasts of fever are a common ailment in some parts of the world. Keep a record of your temperature during your fever. Try to keep cool. Take an aspirin or two and rest. If your body heat rises to about 102° F (38° C), get some medical attention right away.

Whatever the problem, keep a cool head. Think through what you would do if you were at home. If something serious occurs, it's better to see a local doctor than to wait until you return home. They're often more familiar with local and tropical illnesses than your own doctor. Trust them.

If you've been ill overseas, it may be a good idea to register your illness with your doctor at home. Report any medical problems or exposure you had to infectious diseases. If you're on malaria pills, remember to take them for six weeks after coming home. And don't forget that you'll experience some jet lag upon your return, too.

Your short term can be a healthy one. Be sure to encourage your supporters to pray for your health. Trust God. Use common sense. You *can* survive your short term.

Twelve Ways to Ruin a Short Term

Believe it or not, it is possible to have a bad short-term experience. This has little to do with the situation or organization, but a lot to do with the short-termer's attitudes and expectations. To make your short-term experience the best it can be, here's a checklist of what *not* to do:

1. Go it alone. Beware of joining any organization. It could really hamper your style. Pick a country that interests you, find out who the missionaries are, and just show up. They'll love the surprise. Someone with your gifts can usually be used right away.

2. Remember that your purpose is spiritual: you want to win the country to Christ. Go with the highest expectations. Refuse to let menial work such as typing, loading trucks, or working on buildings distract you from your task.

3. Abandon daily prayer and Bible study. Time will go so fast you really won't have time for them. You can usually get all you need from the group devotions.

4. Be organized. Set goals before you go. Plan out your schedule ahead of time and stick to it. Delays, last-minute changes, and impromptu visits and invitations are obstacles to be avoided at all costs. Otherwise, you won't get things done for God.

5. Help the missionaries by pointing out their mistakes. Bring them up to date with the latest missiological trends. Sometimes they can be stubborn, so be sure to win support among the nationals for your views about how the mission should be run.

6. A short term is a perfect time to get involved in a romantic relationship. It may distract you slightly from the work, but it will expose the national Christians to progressive dating patterns from the United States.

7. Don't embarrass yourself by trying to pick up the local language. Remember that English is spoken all over the world, and people want you to help them learn it.

8. Be sure to point out the faults of your team members right away. Time is short, and it may be difficult for people to make the needed changes in their lives if you don't help them from the start. Especially focus criticism on the leadership.

9. Take care not to get dirty or eat the local food. You may miss a few friendly opportunities with "the natives," but you'll avoid any chance of getting sick.

10. Watch out for team members who couldn't raise their full support. They'll try to mooch off you. It will build their faith more if you let them sweat it out.

11. When you report home, castigate your congregation and friends for their lack of commitment, prayer, and giving to missions. This is one of the few times you will have their deferential respect, so make the most of it.

12. After it's all over, remember that as an overseas veteran, you now have an "honorable discharge" that protects you from attempts to draft you into more missions work. Resist the urge to go long-term. A person like you is probably most valuable at home giving lectures on commitment to groups.

Reprinted by permission of **World Christian** *magazine, 1983, Vol. 2, Nbr. 5.*

Expectation Check

Think through your expectations. See what you really think of your upcoming adventure.

Complete the following sentence 15 ways by choosing one ending for each numbered group. Or make up your own sentence endings.

There are no right or wrong answers. Actually, we're just trying to stimulate your thinking. Be honest with yourself. Try to get in touch with some of what you're anticipating and assuming.

On my short term, I will be...

1

_____ eating bugs—raw.
_____ gorging on feasts of native foods.
_____ not eating much at all.

2

_____ the best friend of every national I meet.
_____ cannibalized.
_____ both.

3

_____ returning much more mature and confident.
_____ coming home with my tail between my legs.
_____ never coming home.

4

_____ preaching and teaching 20 hours a day.
_____ spending most of my time lounging around.
_____ not much busier than I am at home.

5

_____ living and working with super-saints.
_____ trekking the jungle alone like David Livingstone.
_____ squabbling with my teammates.

6

_____ sleeping on a dirt floor.
_____ living in the Marriott of Morocco.
_____ having to buy my own bed.

7

_____ seeing hordes come to Christ through me.
_____ wandering around, afraid to talk with strangers.
_____ developing a few good evangelistic friendships.

8

_____ without a bath for two months.
_____ clean, comfortable, and content.
_____ dealing with not having hot water or electricity.

9

_____ bringing home a great slide show.
_____ having my camera stolen.
_____ publishing my journal when it's all over.

10

_____ enjoying the flight overseas.
_____ hijacked and murdered by terrorists.
_____ enduring a near-terminal case of jet lag.

11

_____ able to eat everything, do and see everything.
_____ suffering from malaria, hepatitis, or "the revenge."
_____ dying.

12

_____ losing all my luggage.
_____ on a fun-filled vacation.
_____ getting to tour a couple of cities with my team.

13

_____ gaining the respect of all my friends and family.
_____ making a fool of myself.
_____ having a good, though humbling, experience.

14

_____ sharing the Gospel with dozens every day.
_____ known as the best short-termer in history.
_____ getting my job done, and getting tired.

15

_____ noticed by missionaries and invited to come back.
_____ glad when it's over.
_____ isolated as a radical by the missionaries.

32

My First Night

What the prayer letter didn't say

by Robert Hitching

Robert Hitching has served as director of Reach and Teach Ministries, and has done evangelism in Eastern Europe.

I woke up suddenly. Out of the corner of my eye, I could see a beam of light. *Beam* is probably not the right word. "A muddy shaft" is probably more exact. It came through the crack in one of the curtains. I assumed it was from the moon, yet hesitated to be dogmatic. I had always thought Eastern moons were yellow, and this definitely had some silver qualities to it.

Tonight was my first night on the mission field. To say I felt apprehensive was an understatement.

I played with the beam of light in my mind. When I squinted, it reminded me of the transcontinental flight I'd taken that very day. I sat directly below the movie screen, and the science fiction movie, *Close Encounters of the Third Kind*, was playing.

On the plane I'd struggled with a liberty-discipline problem: should I watch the movie or not? I compromised. I'd watch it, but not rent the headset. Sitting on my right was a hippie on his way east. He'd rolled up a magazine to make a funnel and had one end to his ear, the other to the sound unit on the arm rest.

Now in this bed, it was all so different from what I'd expected. Here I was, infatuated with a moonbeam that reminded me of a movie I wasn't even sure I was supposed to watch. I decided by an act of my will to ignore the beam of moonlight and, since I couldn't sleep, to concentrate on the primary objective of my coming. I rolled over on my back and looked up.

I could hear the gentle swish of the ceiling fan. It was eerie. The fan had been turned on after I'd crawled into bed, and a thought struck me: I had no idea of the distance between me and that ceiling fan. A rush of warmth surged up my neck. I realized that if I sat up suddenly, my missionary career could end abruptly; I could be martyred my first night, decapitated by a Muslim ceiling fan.

I knew I must not panic. Yet I felt the urge to act, like some rebellious instinct was forcing me to sit up. I knew that shoulder-upward, on my side, I'd been safe, so I slowly rolled onto my other side, away from the light.

I made it, filled with relief and accomplishment. I grinned to myself. Then without warning, it appeared. It was terrible—brown, slimy, evil-looking, and just ten inches from my nose.

A cockroach in Nebraska is one thing, but this monster from the Himalayas was sure to be poisonous beyond description. "Please go away," I said in a voice that resembled that of a second grader being surrounded by Hell's Angels from the third grade. Panic set in. Numbly, I managed somehow to regain my initial position facing the beam of light.

As I lay in bed, this night seemed to be the final blow. I couldn't be a pioneer missionary; my calling must have been purely emotional. I couldn't stand the thought of a year-and-a-half like this before I could graduate to an honorable discharge and an administrative desk job at the home base. Eighteen months to go. I estimated that to be more than 2,000 nights.

This was too much. I determined that I could always go to the U.S. Embassy in the morning and borrow the money to fly home. (The hippie on the plane told me about that one.) What a failure—my life career ruined before it started! What would my home church think, or my parents? As I thought of my parents, I began to cry. It was the whiny kind of cry that husbands cry (so I'm told) when they are alone and can't get their own way.

I could see in my mind the kitchen back home—fried eggs, hash browns, and coffee that smelled like the New Jerusalem (as Mom used to say). I decided I needed to read the Bible. If I could somehow make it to the wall and turn on the light, I thought, I'd be safe.

I slowly swiveled my body around and noticed that the cockroach was gone. I carefully lowered my left foot to the ground. Then my foot touched something. It was ghastly, sort of soft and hard at the same time, and clammy.

I thrust myself back onto the bed, breathing heavily. I was desperate. I wondered if the cockroach had injected me with some hideous virus that would send me to a miserable death, preceded by twelve hours of insanity.

The thought left me numb. Then from somewhere came a surge

of the pioneer within me. I decided enough was enough. I determined to make it to the light switch, no matter what.

I pushed myself up, then ducked, realizing that I could have killed myself with the fan. I turned around and ran to the wall. I found the wall—unfortunately, I found it with my forehead—and fumbled for the light switch. It had moved since yesterday. I groped for what seemed like forever, and after finally finding its new location, I turned it on.

Darkness. Panic swept over me again. No light—I'm finished! I then realized I had my eyes closed. I opened them and looked around. The room was much the same as yesterday; the ceiling fan was about 18 feet up. My foot had touched the shoe lying beside my bed.

I picked up my Bible and flicked through to some psalms of comfort. Strange (and yet it shouldn't have been strange), but I felt a sense of release and relief. I turned to some of the Scriptures of comfort in John's Gospel. Gradually, strength began to flood my soul. I began to walk up and down the room, quoting Scriptures and praying for my parents and sister.

After half an hour of prayer, my world began to come into perspective. I looked out the window and saw the beginnings of the early sunrise. Silhouetted against the golden sky was the large dome shape of a mosque. It looked both beautiful and tragic. Something stirred within me: this was why I had come.

I jumped slightly as a knock on the door signaled that it was time for breakfast. At the table, I sat surrounded by stalwart souls who never would have experienced such feebleness on their first night as I had.

"How did you sleep?" my host asked. I looked at the coffee pot. I couldn't look him in the eye.

"Tremendous," I said. "It's so good to be here."

Hypocrite, I whispered to myself as I sipped my coffee.

Going On...

Returning home can be tougher than leaving. You are different and everyone else is different. Going on in your commitment to God's global purpose may mean living overseas for the rest of your life. Or it may mean serving closer to home. Learn how to integrate your short-term experience into your daily life and challenge others to join you in becoming a part of what God is doing in the world.

33

The Homecoming

Coping with reverse culture shock

by Roger Randall

Roger Randall, director of International University Resources for Campus Crusade for Christ and co-founder of the Worldwide Student Network, works extensively with short-term missions around the world.

While you were overseas, something changed dramatically. You did. But you were a little too close to the process to really appreciate the magnitude of the change. It wasn't until your feet touched down on the good old homeland that it hit you.

Suddenly you were struck with the superficiality of life at home. The pace at which you had lived for 20 or 40 years now feels like a fast-flowing river sweeping you along. And everything is so structured. Everything seems to revolve around goals, plans, and schedules. Go to meetings on time. Eat lunch only from 11:05 to 11:35. Endure life ruled by the metal god of the wrist.

But what about people? What about their feelings? Don't these things matter to anyone else?

Speaking of "things," can you believe the "things" in your life? Where did all this junk come from? You thought you needed all this stuff to make you happy. Now it nauseates you.

Actually, it looks like a lot of things at home have changed, doesn't it? Things you always took for granted as "right" may now seem very "wrong"—and you need to go on a crusade to change them. Just little things—like the culture, the Christians, your parents, your church.

Here are some reasons why you feel the way you do and some ways to deal with it.

Levels of Intensity

No one else can share your experience at your level of intensity. When friends ask, "How was your summer?" they're looking for the Cliff Notes edition, not the Amplified Bible version you had in mind. You want to communicate to them the joy you felt at seeing a Buddhist student come to Christ, or the grief you felt as you held a starving child in your arms. You want them to see the sights, whiff the smells, and savor the tastes. Unfortunately, they can't.

After several frustrating experiences in which you pour out your guts and your listener says, "That's an interesting experience. Hey, did you watch that movie on CBS last night?" you may have one of two reactions:

- Withdrawal. "They don't care, and they don't even care that they don't care. Just see if I'll cast my pearls before these swine."

- Attack. "They are going to care, even if I have to keep shoving it down their throats."

There is another alternative. Find a mature Christian friend or your pastor to be your objectivity meter. Tell him or her you want to help infuse a world vision into your sphere of influence. Ask the person to give you feedback regularly. Ask for help to involve others appropriately in your experience.

Changing Back

You feel you've changed, but you find yourself slipping into old patterns. Yes, there were some dramatic changes as a result of your international experience. But, those commitments you made to the Lord this summer may be a little tarnished. The thoughts you thought you'd never think again are now invading your mind. The hard reality is that you still have to live by faith, moment by moment, trusting in the power of the Holy Spirit to live His life through you. There are no shortcuts by taking long plane trips.

Compartments

You may be tempted to compartmentalize and just go on with life as usual. We Westerners seem especially adept at this. We say, "This is sociology, this is chemistry, this is my social life, this is my career. This was my experience last summer. I did my missionary bit, and now it's back to business as usual."

To help avoid this, integrate your experience into every aspect of your life. If your short term hasn't affected your Bible study, your finances, and your social life, you may need to sit down and look at your slides again. Ask the Lord what He wants to build into your character and what new convictions He wants you to take hold of. This may have been a summer project for you, but it's just a part of God's lifetime project to build you into the likeness of Christ, who gave all of His life—not just one compartment—to tell the world of God's love.

Check your I.Q.—your Involvement Quotient. God may have sent you to another culture to prepare you for a lifetime of ministry overseas. If you have a hunch that this might be His plan for you, press on to make that dream happen, but don't sideline yourself from ministry at home.

God sent you overseas, in part that you might become a catalyst for increasing world vision in your church or on your campus. But you'll never catalyze anything if you stay isolated in your own little test tube.

It's time to get out of yourself, get beyond your experience, and get involved. Every organization is in need of leadership. They need men and women who will take on responsibility and trust God for results which bring glory to Himself.

During your short term, you took on responsibility by faith and glorified God in some way. It's likely that you're more ready than ever to lead others. But you'll never know unless you get involved.

Make it a goal to get others involved with you in the very needs you touched. Why not go back next year, taking some of your disciples with you? Remember, Jesus didn't send His disciples off with others; He took them Himself, and showed them how to reach others. He said, "Come with me." He never said, "Go with them."

34

Tell the Story

How to communicate with others
when you return

by Ron Blue

*Ron Blue, professor and department chair of World Missions at Dallas Theological
Seminary, spent a great deal of his life in Latin America.*

I was impressed. Here I was, a rookie missionary talking to one
of the men who had come up with the idea of the Peace Corps. This
man had worked in the White House. He'd conversed with the
President of the United States as informally as we were conversing
now on the steps of the Spanish Language Institute in Costa Rica.

I asked the man, "Now that the Peace Corps has been in operation all these years, has it fulfilled the expectations you had for the
program?"

"Yes it has," he replied, "but there has been an added benefit we
didn't even foresee."

"What's that?" I asked.

"Well, we envisioned the Peace Corps as a way of helping the
world. Actually, the United States has profited more than the
countries we sought to help."

"How is that?" I asked.

"The Peace Corps volunteers returned to the United States transformed," he explained. "They became some of the most dedicated,
productive, visionary citizens of our society."

Fascinating, I thought to myself. *Short-term missions works just like
the Peace Corps. Short-termers can return to become some of the finest
examples of vision and dedication.*

One of the greatest benefits of a short-term experience is probably what happens inside short-termers themselves and how they
can infect their friends and family with a new commitment to
missions. Missions multiplies as short-termers tell their story. And
it's important that they tell it well.

Here are twelve ways to help the communication process:

1. Record stories. During your short term, make a point to remember the details of certain episodes. Write down the sights, sounds, smells, and conversations. You'll be surprised how quickly your memory fades. Without a journal or some written record, you might end up boring folks with a soggy travelogue.

2. Be ready. Don't forget to tell your story in casual conversations. Almost anyone who knows you went somewhere will politely ask, "How was your trip?" Don't give them the limp reply they might expect: "Real great" or "Just super." On the other hand, don't tell them your entire saga. Tell a crisp, one-minute story from your experience.

3. Take initiative. Arrange for settings where you can share your experience. Meet with your pastor to schedule a brief presentation to the church. Get others to help you organize special gatherings or prayer meetings to focus on the mission situation you've known.

4. Speak up. God gave good advice to His prophet Isaiah when He said, "Cry loudly, do not hold back; raise your voice like a trumpet." There's nothing more frustrating than missing an exciting story simply because the volume was too low. Make sure you project your voice so your audience can hear. Speak as clearly as possible. Practice diction.

5. Start strong. The opening sentence ought to have a hook in it with faith that arouses curiosity. Try to create a little anticipation with your opener. Curiosity may kill a cat, but it confirms communication. Never start with an apology or a complaint. Don't say, "I'm really sorry I wasn't able to bring my slides," or "I've been given only five minutes to tell about my short-term experience."

6. Paint verbal pictures. As you move from the opening statement, weave details into the story so that the listener can visualize the scene (the squeaky chair, the smell of incense, children splashing in a puddle, your own feelings at the time). Select descriptions of primary importance. Answer the basic questions: who, what, where, when, and why. Don't overdo it, though. Dress the story for the occasion. Focus on your experience, not on your organization. Be especially careful to use expressions and jargon your audience will understand, because it's common to pick up terms while on a short term that are foreign to your listeners.

7. Illustrate your story. Don't be afraid to dramatize. Act out a conversation. Include facial expressions and verbal inflections. If you use slides, be sure to use them to illustrate. Select only top-quality pictures, and keep them moving fairly quickly and in sequence with the story you want to tell. Don't bore people by merely flashing slides on the screen with a commentary on each picture. In lieu of slides, it's sometimes appropriate to use an object to illustrate a point. One short-termer punctuated an exciting episode of a hunting trip among primitive people by using a blow gun to fire a small dart into the church ceiling. "Every time you look up to see that dart," he concluded, "please remember to pray for the people of Papua New Guinea."

8. Focus on people. Stories that touch the hearts of listeners and move them to a deeper commitment to missions are stories centered on people. Missions is people sending people to reach people. Programs, plans, and policies are important, but they only exist to serve people. Be sure to get "up close," both in stories and slides. Tell all about their thoughts and emotions and, if you take pictures, focus on faces. Everyone likes to see a twinkle or a wrinkle, a tear or a grin, and you can't see those from a distance.

9. Convey important lessons. A good story should have a moral. Well-chosen and skillfully told anecdotes will hold the attention of any audience, but a short-term missionary must do more than entertain. There should be a message. Donald Bray Barnhouse said it well: "Every experience of life can serve to illustrate some biblical principle." Make certain, however, that you don't belabor the point of the lesson. A brief statement will make it clear, such as, "You can't outgive God." Often a biblical quotation will do: "And the greatest of these is love."

10. Accentuate the positive. Try to relate everything in a positive way. There have been far too many woeful tales from suffering saints. Missions has become synonymous with misery. Instead of condemning folks for their evil materialism, challenge them to get in on the tremendous opportunities to invest in the Lord's work around the world. Don't gripe about the trials; glory in the triumphs. When you relate the darker side of circumstances, include a little humor. Instead of bemoaning the isolated conditions of the overseas community in which you served, simply state, "It was not the end of the world, but you could see it from there."

11. Encourage interaction. If possible, give opportunity for questions. The best communication moves on a two-way street. Listen intently to the questions, and do your best to answer as specifically and precisely as possible. You need not feel threatened. You have an answer for every question. One of the answers may be, "I don't know." In the interaction period, be sure to make some supportive comments, such as "That's a good question," or "Did you catch the significance of Fred's comment?"

12. Stop on time. In a culture in which time is of supreme significance, missionary speakers need to contextualize. Short-term missionaries are often relegated to short-time reports. Don't fret. Just give a Reader's Digest condensed version of your story. Whatever you do, don't go beyond the time limit.

As a short-termer about to take off on a life-changing mission, or one who has been out there and come back, don't miss the opportunities to communicate. Who knows? God might use you to ignite the spark within a twenty-first century William Carey, Hudson Taylor, or Cam Townsend. Tell your story.

CHECKPOINT

Evaluating Your Experience

Here are some discussion starters to use with a friend on your way home from your short term. Take several minutes to write out your responses on a separate sheet of paper, then take turns sharing responses. Be sure to pray for each other.

1. The thing I liked best about my short term was....

2. The thing that made my short term most unpleasant was....

3. The most significant lesson God taught me was....

4. The area in my life where I saw the greatest change was....

5. One story that sums up what God did through me is....

6. The biggest challenge I face in returning home will be....

7. The thing I'm most thankful to God for is....

35

Bouncing Back

Some suggestions for the deflated short-termer

by Stanley E. Lindquist and Daniel B. Peters

Stanley E. Lindquist, founder of Link Care Foundation, has spent over 40 years counseling missionaries and helping missions with personnel issues. Daniel B. Peters is currently writing a doctoral dissertation on the cultural history of evangelical spirituality at the Claremont Graduate School.

Turning up the driveway of his home church, Darrin felt a sense of relief to be home. Yet deep down something was bothering him: the lawns were too trimmed, the buildings were too pretty, the pastor's car was too "yuppie" looking. Then, as he waited in the missions pastor's air-conditioned office, looking at pictures of family outings to Disneyland, a seminary diploma, and missions association membership plaques, a sickening feeling began to slowly build within Darrin.

Where was the commitment? Darrin had written home pleading for an offering to help a national pastor get desperately needed surgery, only to hear that the missions budget was spent. That kind of special offering violated church policy.

Where was the Body of Christ when Darrin wrote telling them of his frequent vomiting spells from sheer exhaustion? If he had received one more letter reminding him to leave his concerns at the Cross, he was going to get sick again. How do you leave concerns at the Cross when people in need are standing there stretching out their hands to you? Nobody knew the real story; nobody cared. Darrin told the secretary he had to go.

Six months later, confused and depressed, Darrin came to Link Care Foundation to see a missionary counselor for help getting back into American life.

Often people assume it's easer to reenter after a two-year short term than after being gone for many years. But many missionaries report that the opposite is true. Short-termers feel the shock of adjusting back into the "new-old" culture more, not less. They haven't been away very long, but everything seems to be different.

Short-termers often go overseas with stars in their eyes. They dream of great things happening on the field. They're admired for their dedication. They feel supported by everyone. But usually, they are poorly prepared for the task. They are often surprised by what they find overseas, and they can be even more surprised by what they find when they return.

Reentry problems can be divided into two categories: cultural adjustment and personal reactions.

Cultural Adjustment and Readjustment

Short-termers face the same problems as those who stay longer, but they have to face them and solve them in less time. Most short-term experiences are intense, emotional, and life-transforming. Many young, evangelical Americans live out of a set of assumptions that sorts the world into right and wrong boxes. Seeing throngs of people with physical, emotional, and spiritual needs can easily overwhelm such assumptions of short-termers. The plight of lost people and the problems of missionaries can work together to really shake a person's hope, wither his or her faith, and even reduce the readiness to share love.

Some short-termers have to cope with rather tumultuous experiences. It may be the realities of mass starvation, a national's rejection of the short-termer, or the contradiction between the words and the behavior of a missionary. Few orientation programs help them handle the disappointment, loneliness, depression, and strained relationships they will likely encounter. If these problems don't get worked out during the short term, they can strike back later, just when the pressures of adjusting to home life begin.

Sometimes it is only upon reentry into the home culture that subtle, but serious, shifts in world view are exposed. Often the internal turmoil can lead the short-termers to react to their home culture in a bitter, negative way.

While overseas, short-termers tend to assume that life back home remains the same. It's startling to return and discover change. Friends have married, purchased homes, changed jobs, moved. Any of these changes can create a feeling of insecurity, especially when the expectation is that all at home is secure and stable in contrast to the insecurity and instability on the field.

Personal Reactions

Because of his or her own commitment and sacrifice, the returnee may see friends and others as being uncommitted to the priority of sharing the Gospel with all the world. The person may be right. Because of the fresh exposure to the needs overseas, it becomes too easy to see usual spending habits as lavish, foolish, and unspiritual. The price of a Christian rock tape could support a national missionary for a month. A casual $20 date would feed a family for days and weeks in the country where the short-termer may have been working. A house that cost $100,000 would support the entire mission program.

These seeming excesses can cause a judgmental reaction. Even though nothing is said, the feelings begin to grow and can emerge in quiet, confusing ways. Testimonies in church may show a growing bitterness and disillusionment about the church's commitment.

Often the short-term candidates serve at the bidding of the "real" missionaries. As a result, they may baby-sit or do laundry to free the mothers for the "important" work. Other kinds of seemingly inconsequential work may be expected of the short-termer. This treatment breeds a feeling of unimportance. When those back home display their lack of concern for missions, they reinforce the short-termer's feeling of uselessness. Often short-termers return without a clear vision for the next step in their lives. The pressure of fending off conflicting sets of expectations laid on them is often enough to move them to isolated bitterness.

Ways to Bounce Back

If you are having trouble with reentry shock, here are some practical ways to begin working through it:

1. Remember you aren't alone. Others have gone before you on the short-term missions journey. What you are feeling is probably not unique in the history of missionary emotions. Begin by searching out people who have had a similar experience. Ask them to share honestly what has helped and hindered them during their reentry.

2. Seek objectivity. Go one step further and ask these same people, or others, to be honest about you. If you can muster up the courage, ask someone who in the past has even been critical of you in some way. Ask the person if he or she sees some ways in which your actions, motives, or personality may have contributed to your reentry stress. The goal is to get realistic feedback. You might not get all the realistic feedback that you need if you only ask your mother or your best friend.

3. Face the facts. Get honest with yourself. Take what you've learned from others and face it head on. Although much of what they may say is mere opinion, some will reflect the truth about you. Embrace what is truth. A good help in this process is the book *Telling Yourself the Truth* by Backus and Chapian.

4. Put responsibility where it belongs. No one person is solely to blame. Accept responsibility for your own actions. Your sending agency, your church, your field missionaries, and even the nationals have no doubt partially shaped the way you feel now. Be clear without being judgmental. With a forgiving attitude, cautiously accept your part of the problem.

5. Recognize that change comes slowly. You may not have been all that you wanted to be on the field. You may even be disappointed with how you reacted when you got back. The key is to be faithful today in what God has equipped you to do. Set aside all the rah-rah visions you had of saving the world singlehandedly, and get in the trenches where progress and growth are slow.

6. Check your motivation for going. How do you see the world now compared to your perspective before your mission experience? Make a list of things you learned that will permanently change how you see the world, how you relate to the Church, and how you relate to your peers. Does this list show you anything about God's purpose that you didn't realize initially? Who do you think benefited more from your short-term experience: you or the nationals you went to help?

7. Evaluate your experience. Ask yourself how certain factors contributed to your short-term experience. Regardless of how effective you felt your short-term experience was, ask yourself questions such as these:

- What effect did my job assignment have on me?
- Was the timing of my short term good or bad?
- What effect did the career missionaries with whom I was working have on me?
- Did my support level affect my experience?
- What effect did my expectations have?
- Did I have too many or too few goals?

8. Plan your future. Base your dreams on what God has designed *you* to be. The Body of Christ is dependent on diversity to effectively live and move. Don't let anybody foist onto you their private vision of how you fit into God's plan for the Body. You know that you are to live for God's glory. But is missions the future that God has designed for *you*? Your short-term experience could help you answer that question.

If you honestly accept the mission experience as a permanent part of your life and objectively evaluate it through feedback, you will move back into American culture more smoothly. Deal with the problems of your short term. Whether you move out again from your home culture as a missionary or serve God at home, you'll be much better prepared for whatever He has for you.

"Degriefing"

Rate each statement below from 0 to 5 according to how much you agree with it (5 being highest agreement). The scale is designed to reflect your personal frustration level. If your total score exceeds 20, get some counsel soon. If you score less than 20, you still might want to find someone with whom you can talk. Don't feel left out if you are not feeling any of these frustrations. Not everyone feels disoriented upon reentry from a short-term experience. Keep in mind that this is not a precise measuring instrument. It's designed merely to help you identify areas in which you might need or want some helpful counsel.

_____ People in my home church or group of friends have not seemed very interested in my mission. After a short time, they begin to talk about other things.

_____ Christians seem to be shallow in their faith and not really serious about being World Christians.

_____ I'm feeling shaky about what I believe about God. I saw a lot of suffering—so many people going to hell without a chance. I'm not sure how to put it all together. I'm confused about what I think is important in life. Making decisions is hard.

_____ Missions is really a sham. Missionaries don't really help anyone. They're not as committed as they should be, and they're just as materialistic as everybody here at home.

_____ I'm so tired of trying to get people at home to see the importance of missions that I am physically exhausted.

_____ I am unsure of my motivations for ministry now that I'm back. Why did I really go? Why do I want (or not want) to go back?

36

Growing as World Christians

How to integrate missions zeal into daily life

by David Bryant

David Bryant, author of In the Gap, With Concerts of Prayer, *and* Prayer Pacesetters Sourcebook, *is the founder and president of Concerts of Prayer International–a ministry mobilizing and equipping movements of united prayer worldwide. He and his wife, Robyne, have three adopted children from India.*

On the way back from Manila last summer, I was trying to catch up on some correspondence when a young man interrupted me: "You're David Bryant, aren't you?" Soon after I confessed, a crowd of people surrounded me, as much as they could in the aisle of a 747. They were all members of a short-term missions team returning from a two-month short term in Manila. One burning question brought many of them to my seat: "What do I do now?"

Perhaps this is your question, too. Maybe as you think about living life back home again, you realize that you can't maintain the same patterns, the same relationships, and the same habits that made up your life before. What do you do?

As I've talked to many people in that position, I've received comments like these:

- "I'm scared I won't stay on target."
- "Won't I become imbalanced and too fanatical for my friends?"
- "How do I keep from coming off elitist or super-spiritual?"

Though none of you may use these words, you are really asking: "How do I integrate? How do I allow my newfound commitment to Christ's world vision to mix with everything I am and everything I do in daily discipleship?"

I like to call someone who's going through this process of integration a "World Christian." World Christians are Christians whose life direction has been transformed by a world vision. This isn't a term for frustrated Christians who feel trapped in the missionary movement, who sporadically push a few buttons to say they've done their part. World Christians are heaven's expatriates, camping where the Kingdom is best served. For the World Christian, discipleship must lead into primary ministry with those totally cut off from God's Good News.

I've met many Evangelicals who are overtrained, but underemployed and bored. In light of the tremendous needs, we must move on from our short-term experiences into growth patterns that free us to be laborers at the ends of the earth.

When my wife Robyne and I returned from a summer in India, we knew we had to grow like this ourselves. It had been a hard two months, part of which had to do with the culture and living conditions, and part of which had to do with us. In fact, our little team had a pretty substantial falling-out about halfway through. It took the rest of the trip to try to patch it back together. The whole ordeal reworked some things sadly lacking in our discipleship.

What we realized was that back home, our own approach to spiritual growth—for years, mind you—was so pea-sized in its perspective that, in turn, our view of Christ Himself was also limited. Consequently, in the trauma of culture shock, indigestion, stimulation overload, strange smells, and stranger words, something snapped. It wasn't our team. It was me!

More accurately, my relationship with Christ caved in (thankfully, however, Christ didn't cave in). Why? Because my isolation from previous concern for His global cause had, in the end, warped my vision of Christ Himself. I was ill-prepared to trust Him on the mission field the way a World Christian should, because, simply put, my Christ was too small!

How do we grow as World Christians? How do we grow a world-sized vision of Christ as Lord of our lives? On returning from India, Robyne and I dug into that issue above all others. Here are some practical suggestions we came up with:

1. Wake up every day with a grand intention. When you wake up, tell God, "I am willing this day to seriously explore any new possibilities in Your role for me in Christ's global cause, and to obey immediately whatever You show me." God's primary role for us isn't *going* or *sending*, but being unconditionally *willing*. Tell Him each morning that you are.

2. Let the Holy Spirit give your life a world dimension. He is the Spirit of Christ's global cause. He resides in our lives to give us everything that belongs to Jesus, the Lord of all (John 16:12-15). As He roams throughout the whole earth doing the will of God (Rev.

5:6; John 16:7-11), He remains our constant, most intimate companion (I Cor. 6:17). Be led by Him the way He longs to lead you. (Compare Rom. 8:26-27 with 8:18-25.)

3. Dig into Scripture as a World Christian. I often paraphrase a familiar adage this way: "God has a wonderful plan for the nations, and He loves you and me enough to give us a place in it." Scripture unfolds that awesome blueprint. The more we study it, the more God will show us right where we fit into His plans.

4. Foster prayer as a World Christian. Join with others in prayer for spiritual awakening and world evangelization. One invaluable by-product of pursuing such a prayer agenda is the environment it creates for greater sensitivity to God's voice and for a livelier freedom to obey. (See Acts 13:1-4.) The more we actively pray about the whole counsel of God in world evangelization, the better we'll understand our specific roles, both short- and long-term.

5. Build your world vision. As a minister of the Gospel once put it, God can't lead us into a world mission on the basis of a world vision we don't have. As we couple the blueprint of Scripture with current facts on the opportunities, on people yet to be reached, and on the ministries and people God uses, we'll become better able to respond intelligently and strategically to God's role for us.

6. Explore the possibilities with others. This is no time for loners. Who else in your Christian fellowship desires fuller involvement in the world mission of the Church? Gather regularly with them for Bible study and prayer. Enlarge your world vision by sharing weekly reports. Help evaluate each other's gifts, experiences, and strengths in light of current needs and opportunities. Since Christ calls us into a Body-life, He sends us out in a Body-mission. Therefore we all need to be part of a Body-search as we each seek to determine God's role for us in that mission.

7. Start reaching out now. This may involve cross-cultural ministry in your city. It involves asking yourself the question: "Who can I love for Christ today?" You see, none of us is standing in an unemployment line waiting for a heavenly job-placement counselor to take up our case. There is no unemployment in God's Kingdom. Only as we're faithful to what we can do this day, with the opportunities available to us right where we are, will our Father count us worthy to uncover additional specifics regarding our long-term role in world evangelization (II Thess. 1:11,12).

8. Construct a World Christian lifestyle. In a sense, all of the previous steps help us to do this. We need to actively work at integrating a world vision into everything we think, say, and do, and into the decisions we make along the way. In other words, our current commitment to the cause of Christ will define how we spend our money, what we study in school, what TV programs we watch, who we marry, how we serve our local church, what magazines we read, and how we disciple new Christians.

Even before we've fully determined whether God intends us to be long-term "goers" or "senders," we should be living each day so we know that our lives have counted for Christ's global cause. Learning to live such a lifestyle every day is foundational in learning God's will.

"Every day?" you might ask. Yes. Every day. If you have a spare 15 minutes you can begin right now:

Five: Spend five minutes in personal devotions, discovering some of what Scripture teaches about Christ's global cause.

Four: Spend an additional four minutes reading current world-related literature such as magazine articles or books.

Three: Take three minutes to carry out a mission to the world through intercessory prayer, using what God gave you in the previous nine minutes.

Two: When in conversation with other Christians (such as with your family at the evening meal, in a Bible study group, or in a letter), share for two minutes what God has given you in the twelve minutes of reading and prayer.

One: Finally, before retiring at night, give God one more minute of complete quiet when He can speak to you about who you are becoming as a World Christian, based on the other aspects of your daily discipline.

Fifteen minutes a day. Anyone can do it. Who among us can't find or release an extra quarter of an hour out of twenty-four hours to get equipped for the sake of Christ's global cause and for the billions currently beyond the reach of His Gospel?

Of course, fifteen minutes is only a beginning—a minimum—that may eventually grow into much more. But at any length, it allows you to come to the close of each day, saying with confidence, "I know that today my life has counted strategically for Christ's global cause, especially for those currently beyond the reach of the Gospel."

37

Looking Ahead

Asking the right questions

by Ralph D. Winter

Ralph D. Winter, founder of the U.S. Center for World Mission in Pasadena, California and president of William Carey International University, served for ten years as a missionary in Guatemala.

You know the old saying about putting square pegs in round holes. Well, that old saying started in the military, and I used to think it was a joke. Or that maybe the Army (or the Navy, as was my experience) was simply inept and didn't know what it was doing. Later, I realized that *of course* it put square pegs in round holes. What else do you do if you don't have anything to put in a round hole? You put in a square peg.

In a war, all kinds of people learn new things. The astounding thing about wartime is that many people learn new things they didn't even think they needed to know, or would value, or could ever learn. As a returned short-termer, take care to remember that you're still a soldier in a spiritual war. You may think the big question to ask yourself is: "Did I or did I not have a great experience?" Maybe you even recognize the bigger question: "Is there anything more for me beyond a short term?"

I want to suggest that God wants you to ask yourself an even bigger question: "Could there be something for me other than a career?" In other words, the big question is whether God wants you to pursue a career, or whether He's inviting you out of your career into His cause. The cause is much bigger than any one person's career, and much bigger than any one organization, though it includes many careers and many organizations.

God's cause is called the Kingdom. The war has been won, but battles must still be fought.

God is probably trying to get career-minded Americans to give up their small ambitions (as J.D. Phillips once put it) and accept the fact that a cause—whether it's a physical war between actual nations or a spiritual war between global spiritual forces—always wreaks havoc with career plans. Ask anybody in the military.

I can't forget a statement by the founder of the Navigators, Dawson Trotman: "Never do a job which others can do or will do, if there are important jobs that others can't do or won't do." That means you determine what you do, *not* on the basis of what you'd like to do, want to do, or are prepared to do. It means you choose God's will in terms of what needs to be done because others can't do it or are unwilling to do it. This is, of course, drastically different from the perspective of the average American.

Let's look at the high school senior who has wonderful career plans, with three or four juicy choices. I want to tell you something you won't believe unless you think about it. The average high school senior or college student probably wouldn't like the career he or she *thinks* would be enjoyable.

In other words, it isn't as if the cause of Christ wants to deny you the thing that would really fulfill you most. Rather, the Holy Spirit wants to relieve you of your childish impressions of what the world is like and what you yourself are like. God knows that human beings, without exception, are going to be ultimately fulfilled if they do the thing closest to their hearts. What truly fulfills our hearts is doing God's will.

Therefore, the question to ask after a short term isn't, "Does my peg fit in a missions hole?" That's an inappropriate question, and a dangerous one to ask of your short-term experience.

I have a terrible feeling that thousands and thousands of people come away glad they went and much more experienced than they would have been otherwise, but with a kind of subconscious sense that they can't go back into all that. They think, *If that's what being a missionary is, there's got to be a more efficient way to serve the Lord.* And they're absolutely right. The more efficient way is the longer term. Long-termers live in an entirely different situation.

One of the occupational hazards of the short-term experience is that you're never quite as adjusted as career missionaries. This means the heat is going to be more difficult to deal with and the bugs are going to be more of a problem. Obviously you can't rush out there, set up shop on a very short-term basis, and be as efficient and as protected from special problems as the long-term people.

One thing you *can* do is realize that the things that bother you and get you down are things that long-termers don't just get accustomed to: they deal with them. They get more effective mosquito netting. They find better ways to get safe drinking water, to move around, to live. They become more proficient in the language. As a career missionary, I now realize that most short-termers fall far short of what they could become if they were to stay longer.

The real question to ask after a short term is this: "Am I going to continue in God's cause, or am I going to begin pursuing my own career?" For every Christian who grows up in America, conflict over this issue occurs in the heart. And a deep, profound turmoil remains until we finally realize that what God has in mind for us is better than anything we could have chosen. In fact, there's a famous statement attributed to Jim Elliot that says God reserves the best for those who leave the choice with Him.

Now, this may not be something you can easily accept. It's going to take a step of faith to really be able to put yourself in God's hands.

I have to admit that I'd probably be against short terms if it weren't for the fact that I wouldn't have become a missionary had I not gone on a short term. I'd always thought that missions were the futile, but valiant, activities of a few dedicated individuals who probably weren't accomplishing anything but were at least doing the Lord's will.

I had no idea what I was getting into when a friend called me and said, "They need another young man to go in a car that doesn't have someone in it who can change a tire." At the last minute, I jumped in. This was really a short term—only a three-week trip. We went way down into southern Mexico to the state of Oaxaca. I caused a lot of trouble since I was one of those goof-off kids. I was simply going along for the fun of it—literally just for the ride.

I remember sitting down next to Mexican Indians in an Indian-speaking church in Northern Mexico and being surprised at the very existence of such a thing. I hadn't realized that some Mexicans didn't speak Spanish. We visited different mission stations all down through Mexico; I remember the kind of people who were there. What I discovered were a lot of serious-minded and competent missionaries, and I was impressed by their accomplishments. Seven years later, I decided that was the kind of group I wanted to join.

The question of remaining in the cause is not the question of whether or not you should become a missionary. You can valiantly serve the cause without becoming a cross-cultural missionary. But whatever role you play in the cause, it's crucial to commit yourself to a group. This isn't such a "group-joining" generation, but it's always been quite necessary to put your life in the hands of other people. There's simply no other way to serve in the Body of Christ.

There are very few historical examples of individual missionaries. Even William Carey was flanked by outstanding, consecrated people. The idea that you can go out on an individual pursuit of a career in missions without coming to terms with the need for long-term, difficult-to-achieve, harmonious relationships with other human beings as crotchety as you are is really a very limited idea of reality.

A short term can help you think through this important decision of what kind of organization you want to invest in. The choice of a team to work with is probably your most important choice beyond marriage and your decision to follow Christ. The cause is certainly more than just joining a long-term organization, but your decision to commit to a certain organization must be made in view of the larger cause. What we need terribly in every organization is people who are willing to recognize that their organization can't do the job all by itself.

Your short term can help you answer the most critical questions of your life. Short terms, as I discovered, are full of tremendous excitement, promise, hardship, surprises, discouragement, and challenges. No one ever said short terms are *the* way to win the world, but they sure are a good way to get started.

38

Go for Life

Don't wait for a call to make a move for a career

by Robertson McQuilkin

Robertson McQuilkin, former president of Columbia Bible College and Seminary, spent twelve years as a missionary to Japan.

"What good is short-term missionary work, anyway? You don't necessarily know the language; you don't stay long enough to do anything of enduring value; and you tie up real missionaries' time for months on end." Those were my sentiments exactly. In fact, I probably said something like that twenty years ago. But now, I'm all for short-term missionaries. Why the change?

Well, think about this: acorns aren't all that impressive. Squirrel bait, really. But they do make magnificent oak trees. When I discovered that most new career missionaries in the last decade started as short-termers, I began to applaud the short-term phenomenon. But a troubling thought lurked in the shadows of my mind: true, most career missionaries come by the short-term route, but how many of those short-termers drop out along the way?

With bogus statistics we may be conning ourselves into thinking we have twice as many missionaries now, when we actually don't have many more career missionaries from the United States than before World War II. And an aging lot they are, coming as they did from the battlefronts of the world. They rose to the challenge of saving our world from Nazism, and got toughened up to lead one of the greatest foreign missionary thrusts in Church history. But now they are reluctantly laying down the baton—because there's no one there to grab it and run with it. The future of the missionary enterprise from America isn't bright unless a far larger number of short-termers become career missionaries.

I'm hopeful that as you return to your church after a short-term experience, you'll become a solid World Christian with vision and enthusiasm to inspire others. But inspire others to do what? To do yet more brief stints overseas? Will you, as an ex-short-termer, inspire people to lifetime commitment as career missionaries? Will you go into a career of missionary service yourself?

How can you answer these questions based on your short-term experience? It's a scary business to deal with decades of your life at a time. How do you change your mindset from give-it-a-try to go-for-life?

Part of the answer has to do with expectations. What do you expect to get—or better, to give—in short-term service? In a few cases, a person with the language of the people or with a special skill can make a contribution worth the expense. But for *everyone* who participates in a brief field ministry, there's the potential for a rich education that's well worth the effort of both those who send that person and the missionaries who help him or her learn. Perhaps the most benefit, however, is reserved for those who view the short assignment as a stepping stone to career service.

Start by evaluating your expectations from the beginning. Did you view your short term as an easy way to discharge your missionary obligation or to assuage feelings of guilt? Did you think you could try out a missionary vocation for a brief time? That can be a harmful strategy, like a trial marriage. You can't try out a genuine marriage. To experience what missionary work is truly like without the willingness to bury your bones among the people, and without the hard-won skill in their language, without the commitment to see the job finished, is to experience something different from the real thing.

I spoke with a mission agency director who had seen many new missionaries quit before they had finished one year. I asked him if there was a common cause. "Oh yes," he said, "they're all of the 'Me' generation. The chief consideration is whether or not they are finding fulfillment. When they discover that their expectations are not being met, they head for home."

Perhaps your expectations were geared up for something far more exhilarating than what you experienced. Perhaps you even got a little bored during your time overseas. Beware. You may become one of the "enthused but confused" people I know. They want to be missionaries, but something seems to hold them back. And they don't understand what. They're willing to go, but planning to stay.

This mindset reminds me of a bestseller in the early '80s, *The New Rules*, by sociometrician Daniel Yankelovitch. Through vast research, he demonstrated the commitment of 83 percent of Americans to what he calls the duty-to-self ethic, in which all other values must give way to the supreme value of personal fulfillment. To allow any other value to take precedence is no longer merely dumb; it's dishonest and immoral.

Can it be that we who have heard the instruction of the Master—that life begins with self-denial, and aims at God's fulfillment—have grown to believe that life begins with self-affirmation, and aims at self-fulfillment? Have we redefined what Christ calls "death" to be "life"? Do we cringe from what He calls "life" as if it were death?

Perhaps you want, above all, to commit yourself to the fulfillment of God's purposes in the world. Are you prepared to say "no" to any and every selfish interest that might stand in the way of that purpose? What should you do? How do you break out of your cultural patterns and commit yourself for life as a missionary?

I'm convinced that there's no simple recipe to follow. The ones who make it always seem to press through distractions and take advantage of opportunities of every kind. They seem to be a little pushy and determined about their calling. I've seen very few accidental missionaries.

Paul, the great New Testament missionary, had to press pretty hard to fulfill his vision. As I understand I Corinthians 12:28, the highest calling is that of an apostle, or cross-cultural witness. He says in I Corinthians 12:31 that we should desire the higher gifts. He's basically saying that we should keep on asking God for the higher callings. (The point here is not that missionaries are *superior* to other Christians, but that their *work* is *priority*.) And in the meantime, we should get involved.

Go for it! That's what Paul's command to desire higher gifts implies. In other words, people who stay at home and never lift their sights beyond short-term commitment are making decisions just as surely as those who apply to mission agencies. They are making a decision to stay. You can't just drift. No matter what you do, you're making a decision.

So how do you make decisions that will open up God's great design for your life investment? Get involved, says Paul. Move out in the direction God is moving, and He will open up the way before you.

And if God opens up the way for you to serve at home, then serve Him with all your heart. You can do much to further world evangelization by vigorous witness and involvement in your local church. God values and uses the service of every believer in any occupation.

I'm not pleading for some kind of missionary elitism. You already know that there's no way to improve your standing with God by becoming a full-time Christian worker. If for some reason you can't become a career missionary, please don't count yourself a second-rate Christian who's doomed to a life of mediocrity. Enter into *any* occupation with the same ambition: to glorify God.

Had you asked me when I was eleven years old what I wanted to be when I grew up, I would have replied without hesitation, "A civil engineer." My father had given me an erector set for my birthday, and I was ecstatic. Every free moment was given to building bridges, cranes, and towers. Finally, I asked him what job a grown-up would need in order to play like this all the time. He told me about civil engineering. That became my life's passionate ambition.

But if you'd asked me when I was twelve what I wanted to do, I would have replied, without much enthusiasm, "I don't know. God hasn't told me yet." I'd just made an unconditional commitment of my life to the Lord—the only possible response for a genuine disciple—and no one had to draw diagrams, even for a twelve year old, to show that lordship extended to—indeed, especially to—vocation. But I wasn't obeying Paul's admonition to seek the most urgently needed gifts. For years, I didn't eagerly ask God for *any* ministry. I didn't get involved. I was in neutral, passive, and nothing was happening.

But at age eighteen, things began to change. I really did want my life to count for God's purpose. I began to join Paul in his overwhelming ambition to proclaim Christ where He had never yet been named (Rom. 15:20). I began to witness, to teach children, to preach. No one invited me to preach, so I preached on street corners. But no one stopped to listen, so I preached in the county jail. (They couldn't walk away.) In short, I began to "go for it."

Paul's admonition to seek the higher gifts doesn't mean we should make one request of God and let it go at that. The Greek verb tense means that we are to keep on asking. I asked God to let me be a pioneer missionary, and He made me a high school principal. I just kept asking.

My first problem was health. I had contracted a recurrent condition that disabled me for days at a time, and the doctor said it was incurable. A friend asked if I felt God wanted me on the mission field. "I did think so, and I have long prayed so," I replied, "but look at me lying here incapacitated."

"Would you like me to pray for your healing?" my friend asked. Now, he didn't have any special healing gift; he was just an ordinary college teacher friend. He prayed and I prayed. Nothing happened. So I took another pill to relieve the pain and put me to sleep. Four hours later, I awoke to take the next pill. All of a sudden, I couldn't believe my body. There wasn't a twinge of pain. And for 35 years, my "incurable" condition has left me alone. So we keep on asking.

To be a pioneer missionary and win people to Christ, one must have the gift of an evangelist, the ability to consistently win people to Christ. It was for this I was pleading, because I didn't have it. At least I didn't appear to have it. I would go out on weekends and preach. Sometimes many would turn to Christ. Other times no one would respond. I would return home brokenhearted and plead, "Lord, won't You please give me the gift of evangelism?" I was smart enough to know I would never be a full-sized Billy Graham, but my view of the gift was that I surely would have to be a little model of him.

I learned later that my problem was that my definition of evangelism wasn't biblical. It was very partial, limited to the American model of a mass meeting with an altar call. What I didn't know was that God was answering my prayer all along, making me into the very kind of person He could use in winning Japanese to Jesus. Later I was to discover that my wife and I could move into a Japanese community where there was no church, live among the people, and love them to Jesus. And they would come and come—and form the Church of the living God. He was giving me the gift of evangelism, but I didn't recognize it, so we kept on asking.

We had to keep pushing through all kinds of obstacles to become missionaries. It wasn't just *my* doubts about my adequacy; hardly anyone thought we should go. We even had missionaries tell us to stay where we were. The rationale? "God is blessing you in the ministry you now have."

However, that reasoning didn't seem compelling to me, since I was in the business of hiring people. I sure didn't want to hire anyone God wasn't blessing right where he or she was. It certainly isn't true that God only calls people into missions who can't hack it anywhere else. God's blessing on a person's ministry should be considered the first condition of candidacy for the highest calling.

But my wife and I didn't just need people's approval of our "wild" plans to ignore all our training and experience, leave a great work, and go to untracked stretches of "heathendom." The final decision rested with the mission board, and we'd already tried two. Should we try another? We kept on asking.

The problem, according to one of the boards, was our children. And not their behavior. There were just too many of them—three, with another one on the way.

That's no longer a barrier among enlightened mission boards today, but children have become a barrier to missionary service in another way. Most Evangelicals have adopted one of the key tenets of contemporary secular humanism: environmental determinism. We really do think that parents can—and *must*—create an environment in which their child will turn out "right."

When we pause to think, we know that none of us is good enough or smart enough to create the perfect environment, and that even if we could, it would not guarantee the outcome. Yet still we hesitate to take our children to some foreign land (as if the environment in America were perfect).

And we decide that we'll keep them physically close forever, under our supervision. We'll never "send them away" to a missionary children's school, as if by clinging to them we could keep them safe. What safety is there outside of God's will? And what does it mean that one who doesn't "hate his father and mother...and children" is not worthy of the Lord at all? No, the idolatry of family has the same outcome as every other idolatry: the destruction of both idol and idolater in the end. Far better to entrust our children to follow wherever He may lead.

When we finally concluded that it was God's time, that He'd heard our prayer and was now ready to let us go to the frontier, I went for my physical examination. The doctor came from his office with a somber face. "TB and emphysema," he said simply. I'd been burning the candle at both ends for too long, and now it was time to call a halt. To everything. But we kept on asking. We weren't looking for an excuse to stay; we were asking for the ability to go.

A year later, by the grace of God, we were on a dirty old freighter, preparing to steam out under the Golden Gate Bridge at dawn the next morning. At last God was answering our prayer, giving us our heart's desire. Just then the captain's voice cracked over the loud-speaker, "Sorry to report engine trouble. We will not leave on schedule." He then came and told us personally that we should plan to spend the day in San Francisco so the children could run off some of their energy before the confining weeks ahead. It was to be a traumatic day.

In the evening, we called the children from the playground. It was time to catch a taxi back to the ship. Little Mardi obediently dropped off her self-propelled merry-go-round and stood up to run to Daddy, just as the bar swung around and caught her in the head. We rushed her unconscious little form to the hospital, imagining the worst, as parents will. But before long she came around and seemed no worse for the blow.

We bundled everyone into the taxi and dashed for the ship, only to be met on deck by the captain. "Sorry," he said, "we can't take you with us. We have no physician on board and, should nausea develop, we couldn't tell whether your daughter had a concussion or was merely seasick." So we packed up our cabin luggage and slowly descended the gangplank with deep disappointment, but not despair. We just kept asking.

I'm so glad we did, because God finally got us there. And because of that God-implanted ambition to serve for life, we stayed. He gave us the most thrilling task on earth, sitting down with people every day who had never heard the Good News of life in Christ. We watched broken homes come together, hopeless lives reborn to eternal hope, and a church spring to life. And then another. And another.

Keep on pursuing with all your heart the highest calling, says Paul (I Cor. 12:31). Go for it! Go for life! Going with all your heart is the key to it all. I don't know of anything that will transform you, a short-termer, into a career missionary except a steady pursuing of missionary life—with all your heart.

39

Linking Up for Life

How to become a career missionary

by Kathi Maresco

Kathi Maresco served on two short-term projects to Brazil and France. She and her husband are preparing for long-term church planting overseas.

You've been on a short term, and you've decided that career missions is where you're heading. Like reaching any other goal, this will involve a plan of action. It's easy to get distracted from the task if you stay on home soil, but take the time to become well-trained. There isn't any one prescribed course of action to follow, but here are a few steps you might take:

- **Develop a support team.** These are people who recognize your call to ministry, and who pledge themselves to uphold you. Find a few wise people you can count on to give godly advice.

- **Get rooted in a local church.** It's not enough to attend a church on Sunday mornings. You need to learn what a local church is so you can plant churches on the field. You also need to learn to serve. The best way is to get involved in your local church by carrying out some kind of responsibility. Don't have a home church? Find one soon and give yourself to it.

- **Consider further training.** Don't jump into school without researching what schooling you really need. Don't waste time or money on unnecessary training. Check with mission and denominational agencies as to training you need for the work you're going to do.

- **Travel light.** Don't accumulate possessions. Keep your belongings pared down to bare necessities. This will help you to be flexible and movable.

- **Avoid debt.** It's better to work part time and go to school part time than to amass a debt. It will take longer, but it will keep you from the danger of being distracted from the task while paying off the debt.

- **Keep involved in ministry.** It's easy to get so caught up with participating in God's global plan for the future that you forget to participate in the present. Be involved with evangelism and discipleship now.

- **Determine your strengths and weaknesses.** Ask your spiritual leader what he or she sees as your strengths and weaknesses, and where that person sees you fitting into world evangelization. Evaluate your spiritual gifts and talents to see how they could be used most strategically.

- **Examine career options.** Investigate the needs and situations of countries, people groups, and mission agencies. As you evaluate, think strategy. What is most needed to be done? How will I best meet the needs? What is God's timing for me in meeting the needs?

- **Formulate a plan.** Establish an estimated date of departure for the field. Design specific steps to get there. Assign time blocks for each step, then provide evaluation checkpoints for yourself to determine your progress. Be open-handed with this plan, and allow God to adjust it periodically.

- **Be disciplined.** It's easy to get sidetracked. You must be disciplined if you want to make it overseas. Sitting around won't make it happen. Make a plan and stick to it.

40

More to Learn

Training tips for the long term

by Ted Ward

*Ted Ward, author of **Living Overseas**, worked several years in over 60 countries for Michigan State University's Institute of International Studies. He currently holds the Aldeen Chair of International Service at Trinity Evangelical Divinity School.*

Can you remember the first time you steered a car? For many of us, that exhilarating moment came while sitting on someone's lap. Suddenly, driving seemed easy. What had appeared impossible before, now seemed comfortably in our control.

But there was more to learn. While we focused our childish attention on the tingling twists of the steering wheel, we didn't notice the rest of the details. We didn't see the quick foot trained to respond in a timely and tempered way to the brake and accelerator; the scanning eyes alert to the movement of other traffic and of pedestrians; the skills of starting, parking, and maintaining the machine. When another is handling all those "little things," it's awfully easy to get an exaggerated view of our own competency.

As a short-term missionary, you may have felt this same excitement, even if you only steered part of the missionary enterprise for a brief time. You learned and accomplished missionary work mostly by the feel of it. You might have assumed that, like driving a car, missionary work is just a matter of doing it; there's no way to learn anything more from books or lectures.

Even earlier in life than the encounter with the steering wheel, the bicycle provided some other valuable discoveries. Riding a bicycle isn't the same as riding a tricycle; *that's* a hard discovery.

The bicycle requires balance and a sort of spooky mind-over-matter control that defies explanation. Once you get going, you know the importance of experience. You can't quite capture it in words. It isn't the sort of thing people write books about, nor would you expect to learn it from a lecture. You just do it, that's all.

If you had a positive experience, you might suppose missionary work is as simple as driving a car, or as intuitive as riding a bicycle. So what should you do? Get back as soon as possible and bury yourself in service overseas?

Wrong. Whether driving an automobile or a mission project, there's more to mastery than twisting a wheel or traveling to the other side of the world. Only a grinch would take away a youngster's excitement over that first moment with the wheel, but somehow the newcomer must be brought to reality; the successful short-term missionary must remember that there is more to learn.

It's easy to assume that the day-after-day short-term experience is the same thing as the year-after-year missionary experience. While the short-term missionary may come to understand something of missionary work and make useful contributions, the long-term responsibilities and logistics of negotiating, initiating, persevering, evaluating, and replanning remain mostly hidden. Keeping one's wits as a career missionary requires a great deal of preparation and training.

The old proverb says that "a little knowledge can be a dangerous thing." Indeed, sophomores generally critique professors and parents with equal vigor. Suddenly they perceive themselves as smarter than everybody else—and willingly share brilliant thoughts with anyone who will listen.

The crucial issue usually boils down to whether the best of the short-term missionaries are willing to discipline themselves to obtain the additional training they will need. Then they can return to missions with both heart and head prepared for the realities of long-term ministry.

Most short-term missionaries need further training: deepening theological knowledge and sharpening career skills.

Biblical Foundations

Ground yourself in biblical and theological studies if you expect to handle the Word of God with care and competency overseas. The possibilities of service in missions aren't restricted to those with a particular form or set amount of education, but most sending organizations and denominational boards insist on a year or more of formal biblical and theological training.

Today, many prospective missionaries ask the question, "Do all missionaries need theological education, or only those who are going to preach and teach?" This issue particularly concerns those who feel called to ministries of social service, welfare, disaster relief, and certain specialized technical operations such as radio, aviation, and literacy teaching.

Mission executives as well as missiologists (those who study and teach missions) agree almost unanimously that everyone in missions—including spouses—needs grounding in biblical and theological studies. Those who organize and administer missions quickly note that individuals who lack an adequate grasp of theology are often misguided in their efforts, and create problems that inhibit the mission. Missions experts typically urge all those who engage in a mission ministry (even those who serve as technicians and specialists in support of "regular" missionaries) to enroll in one to three years of theological studies.

Preferably, you should organize such learning so that it provides both a foundation for ministerial skills and a knowledge base for disciplined use of Scripture. You can best gain such a learning experience through a ministry degree program in a theological seminary; one which maintains a fundamental commitment to the centrality of the Bible as God's truth.

This advice doesn't rule out the validity of self-taught handling of the Scriptures as a basis for service. But such highly disciplined, self-guided, or informal learning of theological foundations is rare, especially among those who have devoted most of their studies so far in life to classical academic subjects. Generally, it works much better to put all of the biblical and theological studies into a degree program and go at it just like any other important academic effort.

Career Skills

You'll also need to train yourself for the vocational tasks and skills of your career. If you're heading for the common role of "general missionary," this vocational training may overlap with the pastoral and ministerial skills you'll learn in your theological training. But for the specialist, the technician, and the bi-vocational (tentmaking) missionary, the necessary career skills may require an additional and similarly demanding body of knowledge. The most demanding case of all, of course, is the medical missionary, who more often than not is close to 35 years old before completing both a medical and theological education.

Here again, the time required may frustrate you, especially in light of your eagerness to get back to the field. If only there were responsible shortcuts! But there are none. Cutting corners in a zealous effort to get to the field quickly for a long-term assignment doesn't work.

I want to give a word of warning to those who feel called to become "tentmaking" missionaries. The quality of your workmanship and the integrity of your service will reflect positively or negatively on Christ, whom you claim to represent. You shouldn't approach the vocation that will sustain your livelihood overseas as a sort of necessary evil. Your vocation demands your best. The work of Christ, especially in your case, will depend on it. So be a tentmaker—but make your "tents" well, and trade them fairly.

Serve Well

It's one thing to be willing to serve; it's another thing to serve well. Fervency and youthful exuberance can work against effective ministry. Eagerness is an inadequate substitute for training. The best combination is fervency plus competency.

People who don't like to wait often quit. They start out quoting Paul's encouragement to Timothy, "Don't let anyone look down on you because you are young..." a sort of all-purpose salve for bruised greenhorns. But they ignore the rest of Paul's statement, which is vital: "...but set an example for the believers in speech, in life, in love, in faith and in purity" (I Tim. 4:12). The solution for an inexperienced person lies not in demanding that the critics stop criticizing, but in developing greater competency.

To honor Christ, the Christian must perform responsibly. Make no mistake about it; proper education and pertinent training for the development of appropriate skills can make a big difference. Incompetency, shoddy performance, and irresponsible behavior are unworthy of Jesus Christ. If a person says that Christ is Lord, his or her life ought to reflect that statement.

If the word *Master* is to be anything more than a pious catchword, it has to mean that you're willing to go to any length to develop the gifts of the Holy Spirit and to place them into active service on the altar of living sacrifice before the holy God.

There *is* a difference between short-term and long-term missionary service. The former consists of a sort of tethered experience in someone else's operations; the latter involves structural responsibility, which requires far more preparation.

It's been said, "the Peace Corps provides two years of experience that will last a lifetime." The short-term missionary venture is also valid in itself. But when it can be followed by effective preparation for ministry and service in the international community, it becomes a temporal experience with eternal consequences.

Should I Go On For Life?

To help you evaluate whether or not you are motivated and ready to become a career missionary, complete each of the following ten sentences. You may have more than one response per sentence.

1. I am _____ going for life.
   _____ open to the idea of
   _____ feeling guilty about not
   _____ avoiding the issue of
   _____ already committed to
   _____ already making specific plans about

2. The best model for me in becoming a lifetime missionary is probably...
   _____ my grandparents.
   _____ the missionary that I met during my short term.
   _____ no one I know. I don't have any good models.
   _____ other: _____

3. My life plans are mostly shaped by...
   _____ a desire for nice things and security.
   _____ a desire to glorify God.
   _____ my college major or career goals.
   _____ the short term that I just went on.
   _____ the unfinished task of world evangelization.

4. My inventory of life goals includes...
   _____ people coming to Christ through me.
   _____ things like a good education, position, and home.
   _____ becoming famous.
   _____ raising a great family.
   _____ leaving a mark on the world.
   _____ other: _____

5. I'm undecided about becoming a lifetime missionary because...
   _____ I had a bad time overseas.
   _____ God has not yet called me to do so.
   _____ I don't know how.
   _____ I know that I'm not qualified.
   _____ I'd like to try some other things in my life.

6. The thing that might stop me from becoming a missionary is...
_____ parents or other family members.
_____ I hate raising support.
_____ I don't want to go as a single person.
_____ I'm too far in debt to go soon.
_____ I have poor health.

7. When I say God is leading me to be or not to be a missionary, I mean that...
_____ He has spoken directly to me.
_____ I'm hearing His voice through others.

8. If God let me do anything that I wanted for His sake, I would...
_____ work in my home church
_____ start my own ministry.
_____ be a missionary for the rest of my life.
_____ work in the secular field, reaching others for Christ.

9. On the mission field, I could see myself...
_____ doing evangelism.
_____ discipling young Christians.
_____ teaching Bible school.
_____ serving in the medical profession.
_____ serving in a tentmaking capacity.
_____ teaching through Bible correspondence courses.
_____ doing community development.
_____ other: _____

10. If I really intended to go overseas, right now I should...
_____ start paying off my school debt.
_____ get some biblical training.
_____ reach out to those already around me.
_____ begin explaining by goals to my parents.
_____ get more involved in my local church.

INDEX